SEEING CLEARLY
PRINCIPLES, PEOPLE, AND PURPOSE

FIRST STEPS FOR LEADERS

by
DR. MICHAEL B. HOYES

ISBN:1507833199
ISBN-13:9781507833193

DEDICATION

May this be said about me, not only for this book, but also in life: "*I have fought the good fight, I have finished the race, I have kept the faith*" (2 Timothy 4:7, NIV). To the professors, particularly Dr. Gary Oster, thank you for your steadfast counsel and prayer. To my Regent University 2011 DSL Cohort, you have enriched and encouraged me as we journeyed together, and I pray blessings upon each of you now and always. To my family, and most especially my wife, Claudia, thank you for putting up with my absences from our family life to which I am eager to return. To you, dear reader, may this text increase your ability to see clearly and lead well!

CONTENTS

FIGURES

TABLES

FORWARD

The world is now one hurried, turbulent global marketplace filled with rapidly changing ideas, organizations, and products. The limited skillset required of successful leaders in the 20th century is largely insufficient to lead in the 21st century. Because the gap between success and permanent corporate dissolution narrows each moment, every leader (regardless of position on the organizational chart) needs new, adaptable skills and attributes to support the systemic cornerstones of principles, people, and purpose.

As former Herman Miller, Inc. CEO Max DePree noted, "The first responsibility of a leader is to define reality..." This idea ably summarizes the thrust of the new book by Michael Hoyes entitled, Seeing Clearly: Principles, People, and Purpose - First Steps for Leaders. Although it is an important text for bachelor's and master's level students, it is also helpful both to the experienced leader and aspirational leader just emerging. Chapter summaries, questions to ponder, and additional resources enhance the value of the text. This book is not a musty academic tome nor is it a quick five-step self-help cookbook for becoming a better leader. Instead, Dr. Hoyes invites readers to dig deeper for a close-up examination of the important concepts underlying successful modern leadership.

"Seeing clearly" is not a short-term method that allows leaders to discern obvious threats and opportunities. The book utilizes contemporary examples to plainly demonstrate and explain how concepts can become actionable. People and their personal values are the center of the leadership world. Seeing clearly involves all of the senses, the heart, and wisdom. It logically examines the all-important "why" behind the "how" of leadership literature. Most importantly, seeing clearly requires knowing why the organization exists and where it currently stands in relation to that purpose. It implies a responsibility for personal humility and continuous vibrant communication to and from followers and peers.

Dr. Hoyes is well suited for this consideration of the "deep things" of leadership. A decorated Air Force fighter aviator (call sign "Yama"), strategist, and officer, Dr. Hoyes has practiced leadership where it matters most: in the heat (and fog) of battle. He continues to be a highly successful leader in business, church, and community. As a committed Christian, Dr. Hoyes wrote this book from an unapologetically Christian worldview, giving it a richness and texture not usually found in leadership books. He ably demonstrates the way in which faith is an integral element of leadership. Seeing Clearly acknowledges the complexity and challenge of leadership practice, yet underscores the importance of treating employees as "hired hearts" instead of "hired hands."

As leadership experts Larry Bossidy and Ram Charan have said, "Wishful thinking, denial, and other forms of avoiding reality are deeply embedded in most corporate cultures. But what's been tolerated in the past can't be tolerated in this new environment. The price for failing to confront reality is simply too high." Seeing Clearly: Principles, People, and Purpose - First Steps for Leaders is an important practical antidote to the leadership myopia, which yields that dire prognosis.

Dr. Gary Oster
Professor of Innovation & Entrepreneurship
Regent University School of Business & Leadership
Virginia Beach, Virginia

Chapter 1

WHY IS SEEING CLEARLY SO IMPORTANT IN THE CONTEXT OF LEADERSHIP?

"Why do you look at the speck in your brother's eye but don't notice the log in your own eye? Or how can you say to your brother, 'Let me take the speck out of your eye,' and look, there's a log in your eye? Hypocrite! First take the log out of your eye, and then you will see clearly to take the speck out of your brother's eye."
(Matthew 7:2-5)

Imagine if you can, what it might have been like for you in the womb, and then suddenly, birth! You need to learn how to breathe...the light is so bright, the outside air is so cold ...until now you were used to the enveloping comfort of a home around 98.6 degrees. There are smells, but you may not be aware of them as of yet. There was some pain involved in the birth process you have just been through, pain that, to date, you have not experienced. But now, sounds are clearer...and louder, much louder. And your eyes...those bright lights...you can see, but not clearly. That will come with time, as will your ability to recognize those who will take care of you for the next few decades. We do not get to skip childhood to arrive at adulthood; we must develop into the man or woman we are now. This is the same for leadership and specifically our understanding of seeing clearly. This concept is something that can be learned, but it will take time and effort, and yes, there may be pain involved.

If you are a busy person, perhaps in a middle leadership position, this work is meant for you. You may suffer, as do I, with being so busy *doing* that you sometimes fail to pause to understand why. Hence, little reflection occurs in your harried existence.

Perhaps you are an organization's senior leader (e.g., CEO or president), wrestling with the requirements of organizational change in our increasingly interconnected and interdependent world. In this new world, your competition may reside across town or across the globe. Within these pages, you will find arrows to place within your quiver. Perhaps, like leaders below you in your organization's hierarchy (e.g., vice presidents, chief information officer, directors, managers), you have not taken much time to reflect, and the thought of a retreat to ponder these questions may have been out of the question (one may ask, "Why so?" but we will address this later). Within the pages that follow, you will have your opportunity to consider these matters and, more importantly, *apply* them in your environment.

For those entering leadership positions, this is for you as well. As you develop and grow, you will experience good and poor leaders, but you may not have a frame of reference to understand why they are so deemed. Of course, your desire is to follow the path of the good leader, but what does that mean? "The use of the word good here has two senses; morally (ethically) good and technically good or effective" (Ciulla, 2004, p. 13). The focus of this work is on the former. The challenge will exist for all across the leadership continuum to do some self-examination, as Socrates stated, "an unexamined life is not worth living" (Guinnes, Mooney, & Thorp, 2000, p. 79).

It is the goal of this work that each of the above types of leader find insights into seeing clearly, and that they might understand just how important it is to see clearly. Though the reader can feel free to advance to topics of interest, this work is arranged in a sequential order intentionally—earlier sections are foundational to those that follow. A key argument of this entire work is that the individual's leadership abilities (and also the organization's) grow from the inside out, as implied by the verse that began this chapter. There appears to be a sort of chronology, whereby: "The leader's foundational values yield beliefs, [which lead to the leader's] intentions to behave…and actual behavior. [These leadership] behaviors help form followers' attitudes that affect how they behave" (Winston, 2002, p. iv).

A primary focus of this work is a view of leadership as a moral relationship, which is a values-based model, in contrast with a performance or competency-based model. These are competing models for examining leadership. Organizational behaviorists at Yale University tracked more than 10,000 Army leaders from their entrance into West Point through graduation and well into their careers, representing 20% of West Point's living graduates. They determined:

> Those who lead primarily with internal, intrinsic motives performed better than those with external, instrumental rationales for their service—a common finding in studies of motivation. We were surprised to find, however, that those with both internal and external rationales proved to be worse investments as leaders than those with fewer, but predominantly internal, motivations. Adding external motives didn't make leaders perform better—additional motivations reduced the selection to top leadership by more than 20%. Thus, external motivations, even atop strong internal motivations, were leadership poison. It is important that talent managers and executive decision makers do not allow external consequences of leader development to become external motivations among organizational leaders. (Kolditz, 2014)

The above observation presents you with the first glimpse of what we mean by "seeing clearly," and where your focus should begin. Note that internal motives, at least in the sample observed, was a better indicator of future performance than either external motivations or even a blend of internal and external motivations. Those who were internally motivated saw clearly to remove the rods from their eyes and experienced excellent results as they began to lead others. To enable us to understand how seeing clearly will be applied to principles, people and purpose, let us take a closer look at this concept.

"Seeing Clearly"—What Does it Mean?

Several decades ago, as the United States military sought views of how to best combat adversaries, Air Force Colonel John Boyd developed the OODA Loop. This was not some tricky method of maneuvering an aircraft inflight to defeat an opponent. Rather, OODA means: "Observation, Orientation, Decision, and Action" (Hammonds, 2002), and Loop implies that following the fourth element, action, the process begins anew. As an approach, it was deemed appropriate not only for individual aircraft maneuvering (in other words air-to-air combat), but also when developing tactical or strategic planning. Likewise, it has gained traction in the business arena.

The first step of the OODA Loop, germane to this discussion, is to observe, or in the vernacular of this work, to see clearly. As we continue to develop this concept, you will understand that being able to see clearly facilitates our ability to apply speed, flexibility, integration, and innovation to whatever challenges arise. It concerns not only the leader's view of the external environment, but also the internal environment of the organization. And yes, it is also applicable as a tool for self-reflection. We will see that it becomes not only the leader's responsibility to see clearly, but it is also the obligation of the entire organization—including each and every follower—to do so. This will enhance the creative abilities of the organization. Why is this important? Because "every organization wanting to stay competitive in an innovation-driven economy needs creativity from every one of its people" (Burkus, 2014, p. 48). To have unity of purpose, which we will discuss at length in a later chapter, the organization needs unity in what is being observed or seen, as well as in visualizing the way forward. Now, all of this observation takes time. "Learning to see slow, gradual processes requires slowing down our frenetic pace and paying attention to the subtle as well as the dramatic" (Senge, 2006, p. 23).

Your parents, at some point, probably admonished you to "look before you leap," and with good reason. You need to understand the environment and certainly what you are jumping into prior to taking that one small (or large) step. Two automotive examples demonstrate the perils of not seeing clearly. These perils help form the "logs" mentioned in the Matthew verse above. The first peril results from distraction, which results in not focusing on the right thing. Every driver should be aware of the potential danger with being distracted—even for five seconds, such as what may occur during texting. Traveling at 60 miles per hour, it only takes five seconds to go 400 feet, which is more than the length of a football field – all while the driver has not been observing what is in front of the car!

The U.S. Department of Transportation reports that in 2012, the number of people killed in distraction-affected crashes was 3,328, while the number injured was 421,000 ("What is distracted driving?," n.d.). Distraction is, therefore, something that needs to be taken very seriously, both while driving and within your organization.

There is a second peril; one caused by not knowing where to look, which again, results in not wisely discerning the environment. I spent about four years living in England during the 1980s. Periodically, there were news reports of pedestrian tourists killed simply because though they looked, they were not looking in the proper direction. In the United States and a preponderance of nations, one drives on the right side of the road, whereas in England (as well as other locations) one drives on the left. A "right-side-of-the-road-minded" pedestrian might, therefore, look to their left for oncoming traffic when stepping out into the street, only to be struck from their right. Due to habit, they did not look in the proper direction for their safe transit across the thoroughfare. Of course, all over the world, this particular peril of not knowing where to look has been exacerbated by the use of headphones while walking, where the wearer seems oblivious to their surroundings. As with distraction, knowing where to look also needs to be taken very seriously.

In summary, as used for the remainder of this work, seeing clearly (SC) is not merely an ocular event. In fact, SC may rely on many senses, and it also includes wisdom. Even more, SC involves your heart. It implies a deep, holistic understanding of the issue with openness (as contrasted with bias) to receive unfiltered information. It requires attentiveness and observation of the correct things based upon the situation. It requires active thought and engagement from you. SC may even evoke passion, which emanates from your heart.

Seeing Clearly—Leaders and Leadership

Since our discussion concerns SC and leadership, with our understanding of SC in this framework, it is reasonable for us to turn to leadership and leaders in this context. Two professors at Regent University, Winston and Patterson (2006) conducted a study uncovering "over 90 variables that may comprise the whole of leadership" (p. 6). Their efforts led to what they describe as an integrative definition of a leader:

A leader is one or more people who selects, equips, trains, and influences one or more follower(s) who have diverse gifts, abilities, and skills and focuses the follower(s) to the organization's mission and objectives causing the follower(s) to willingly and enthusiastically expend spiritual, emotional, and physical energy in a concerted coordinated effort to achieve the organizational mission and objectives. (Winston & Patterson, 2006, p. 7)

Continuing to explore this idea of leader and leadership, other scholars define leadership as a *process*; in other words, what the leader does: "Leadership is the process of influencing others to understand and agree about what needs to be done and how to do it, and the process of facilitating individual and collective efforts to accomplish shared objectives" (Yukl, 2010, p. 8); "Leadership is a process whereby an individual influences a group of individuals to achieve a common goal" (Northouse, 2010, p. 3)

Whether one choses to view just the definitions of leader or leadership, we can see that leading involves people, whereby one (or a group) influences others to achieve some sort of goal, mission or purpose that is mutually agreed upon. The implications for those desiring to lead are that they must clearly see the shared objectives, mission or goal (which will be discussed in detail within our "Purpose" section); can chart a path toward that goal; and can convince others to see and join them in attaining the goal. Here's the good news and the purpose for this work: "We can all learn to lead" (Sinek, 2011, p. 1). Thus far, we've explored this concept of leadership in an academic fashion. How might it play out in the real world?

Dr. Ben Carson, within his book, *America the Beautiful*, describes his life as a young boy. Within that text, Carson recounts experiences he and his brother faced in a fatherless home. I will let his words speak for themselves:

She was almost always out working, trying to provide for us as best she could. Consequently, we almost never had anyone around the house to referee our disputes or hound us to do our chores. How was Mother able to establish effective rules in such a chaotic situation? Although we got into a fair amount of trouble at home, there never were any serious incidents because we had

4

guidelines that governed our behavior in the absence of an authority figure. Mother was smart enough to realize that if she simply imposed rules on us, we were unlikely to follow them; therefore, she involved us in the rule making. We all had a say in who would do the dishes, who would sweep the floors, who would warm the food, who would take out the garbage, and so on. We also agreed upon the punishment for not carrying out one's duties and the rewards for doing a stellar job. This system of governance was well defined and well accepted, so there was almost no trouble. I am frequently asked why Curtis and I obeyed our mother when sometimes we didn't see her for an entire week. The answer is quite simple—they were not just *her* rules, they were also *our* rules, for ownership of an idea makes cooperation with its tenets much more likely. (Carson, 2012, pp. 29-30)

Let us review those final words again: "Ownership of an idea makes cooperation with its tenets much more likely." The young boys were led by their mother to own the idea, which made their cooperation much more likely. This is what is meant within the academic definitions by "influencing people to achieve a goal or mission that is mutually agreed upon." As a family unit, they understood their purpose, goal, or mission. This translates to understanding and agreeing to the why of their small organization, which informed how they would perform their responsibilities and what would result. Her actions led her sons to see clearly and join her in attaining the goal of an orderly abode. Did Carson's mother demonstrate the leadership to which we are discussing? Yes indeed! This is why this work applies to not just the senior corporate leader, but to leaders in all domains, even those who may not initially think of themselves as being in a leadership position.

Clearly then, leadership involves influencing others. Without others (in other words, followers) and without influence, leadership would not exist. The objective of this influence is to convince, which requires communication. Without a purpose, there is no need for leadership, followership or an organization for that matter. The phrase "shared objectives" implies a purpose for the leader's influence, and informs why the organization exists. One scholar states, "Followers and leaders both orbit around the purpose" (Chaleff, 2009, p. 13). People and purpose are therefore essential to an organization's existence. It is for this reason they each comprise chapters within this work.

When we speak of influence, we do not mean coercion. "Coercion means influencing others to do something against their will and may involve threats and punishment" (Northouse, 2010, p. 9). Classic coercive leaders include, among others, Adolph Hitler in Germany, Jim Jones in Guyana, and David Koresh in Waco, Texas. The leadership we speak of here is not gained by coercion, rank, or status. It is a result of "a common purpose pursued with decent values…the heart of the healthy leader-follower relationship" (Chaleff, 2009, p. 13). This introduces another concept we will spend quite a bit of time reviewing in the next chapter, the concept of values. Suffice it to say, "one of the most important jobs organizational leaders do is instill and support the kind of values needed for the company to thrive" (Daft, 2010, p. 373). These points are marvelously captured within General John M. Schofield's address to the graduating class of 1879 of the United States Military Academy at West Point, as he discusses discipline as an aspect of leadership:

The discipline which makes the soldiers of a free country reliable in battle is not to be gained by harsh or tyrannical treatment. On the contrary, such treatment is far more likely to destroy than to make an Army. It is possible to impart instruction and give commands in such a manner and such a tone of voice as to inspire in the Soldier no feeling, but an intense desire to obey, while the opposite manner and tone of voice cannot fail to excite strong resentment and a desire to disobey. The one mode or the other of dealing with subordinates springs from a corresponding spirit in the breast of the commander. He who feels the respect which is due to others cannot fail to inspire in them respect for himself. While he who feels, and hence manifests, disrespect towards others, especially his subordinates, cannot fail to inspire hatred against himself. ("John McAllister Schofield quotes," n.d.)

General Schofield noted that the manner in which a leader influences the subordinate "springs from the heart" of that leader. This manner is something that dwells inside the leader that is brought to light by the leader's actions (or words). Further, how the subordinate is treated (influenced) will have a direct bearing on how the leader (and the organization) is viewed. This will likely impact how well the subordinate performs, and as we will discuss later, how that employee interacts with customers.

When we speak of influence, we also do not mean manipulation. Here are some examples of common manipulation efforts we see (but may not realize) on a day-to-day basis:

- *Price* – as an organization, drop your price low enough and people will buy from you;
- *Promotions* – "buy one get one free," such a common manipulation, we sometimes forget we are being manipulated in the first place;
- *Fear* – when employed, facts are incidental, it motivates us away from something horrible;
- *Aspirations* – the opposite of fear, they tempt us toward something desirable; and
- *Peer pressure* – "over a million satisfied customers," and celebrity endorsements work because we believe others know more than we do. (Sinek, 2011, pp. 17-25)

Now, if you can agree with this premise of leadership being a process, surely you would also agree that a process must begin somewhere, correct? This understanding of the starting point, the ability to see it clearly, is just as important as where the organization needs to go. Hence, "the first responsibility of a leader is to define reality" (DePree, 2004, p. 11). The leader must describe for followers not only the internal environment, but the external one as well. The leader must have a strong understanding of why the organization exists (its purpose) and where the organization is (relative to that purpose) in order to chart where it needs to go. This implies the ability to clearly see as we have defined that term. Again, let's look at a practical example.

During night flying training for United States Air Force navigators, the student navigators and their instructors are physically located in the back of a large training aircraft. Their goal (purpose or mission) is to direct the pilot along a particular flight path, transiting many states and abiding by a plethora of Federal Aviation Administration rules of flight, to bring the aircraft to a planned destination on time. Once the aircraft levels off at cruising altitude, the first thing the students need to do is determine where they are. To do so, they each use a sextant, navigational tables and charts to map the positions of stars or other heavenly bodies (such as Earth's moon or one of the planets). Using triangulation, they make that positional determination, understanding where they are. Then, using other flight aides, they determine what course they need to fly to get to the desired destination. As with an organization, the external environment may contain winds or other hazards that could alter the ground track and ground speed of the aircraft. Unless correctly observed and adjusted for, these external forces could result in not arriving at the desired destination or arriving at the destination too early or too late. To fly, the students must clearly see (comprehend) where they are, what forces are acting upon the aircraft, and then chart a course to include airspeed, which would be communicated to the pilots flying the aircraft. As with an earth-bound organization, this is not a one-time effort. The students must periodically monitor where they are to be certain they are not being "blown off course" from where they want to go, and of course, provide updated information to the pilots. This analogy holds true for organizational leaders at all levels.

At this point, depending on your status, you may be thinking to yourself, "I am not the CEO of an organization, nor am I navigating an aircraft, so how does what is being stated affect me?" Again, because this text is designed for all types of leaders, we should take a moment to contemplate the two basic forms of leadership. They are called *assigned leadership* and *emergent leadership*. Assigned leadership is "based on occupying a position in an organization" (Northouse, 2010, p. 5). This is where your CEO fits, as well as other positions of leadership in your company's organizational chart. However, in the day-to-day activities of your company, there are probably many other people—perhaps even yourself—that demonstrate leadership in a particular setting or situation. "When others perceive an individual as being the most influential member of a group or organization, regardless of the individual's title, that person is exhibiting emergent leadership" (Northouse, 2010, pp. 5-6). Here we recall our definition of leadership as we see, yet again, the concept of influence within this last definition. Though you may not have a designated or assigned position of leadership, there may be conditions where you are the most influential and are in actual fact, an emergent leader, and influence can be regarded as "the essence of leadership" (Yukl, 2010, p. 408). Colleen C. Barrett, president emeritus of Southwest Airlines, put it succinctly: "We want all our people to realize they have the potential to be a leader" (Blanchard & Barrett, 2011, p. 2). This being the case, everyone within the organization needs to see clearly!

Seeing Clearly—What About Followers?

It should be a statement of the obvious—one that all leaders should see clearly—leadership cannot exist without some sort of followership. We made mention of this fact previously. Leadership and followership may be viewed as opposite sides of the same coin forming "a symbiotic relationship where leadership acknowledges and respects the professional, knowledgeable, experienced, skilled, and trustworthy contributions of followership" (Prilipko, Antelo, & Henderson, 2011, p. 79). Research indicates, "Leaders contribute on the average no more than 20% to the success of most organizations. Followers are critical to the remaining 80%" (Kelley, 1992, p. 7). We spend some time reviewing followership because, "no serious student of leadership can any longer ignore its essential counterpart" (Chaleff, 2009, p. xiii), the follower.

When we view leadership from the eyes of the follower, we see, "followers determine not only if someone will be accepted as a leader, but also if that leader will be effective" (Kelley, 1992, p. 13). Let's briefly examine some leadership style definitions to see this point clearly demonstrated. The leadership styles, themselves, are not the focus of our discussion, though you will undoubtedly read about them in various other domains. The point, here, is the impact the follower has on the leader's style, no matter which style the leader employs. In each of the definitions, it is the follower who reacts and, to some degree, actually defines the leader's style:

- <u>Follower attribution of charismatic qualities to a leader is jointly determined</u> by the leader's behavior, expertise, and aspects of the situation,
- <u>Transactional leadership motivates followers by appealing to their self-interest</u> and exchanging benefits,
- <u>Laissez-faire leader shows passive indifference about the task and subordinates,</u>
- <u>Transforming leader appeals to the moral values of followers</u> in an attempt to raise their consciousness about ethical issues and mobilize their energy and resources,
- <u>Servant leader is about helping others</u> to accomplish shared objectives by facilitating individual development, empowerment, and collective work <u>consistent with the long-term welfare of followers</u>. (Yukl, 2010, p. 275-277)

Again, in each of the above definitions of leadership style, we note how the follower's reaction to some degree defines the style of the leader, which would, in turn, have an impact on the organization. If you still do not believe that a follower can have great organizational impact, look no further than to the author of the United States Declaration of Independence:

Most people think of [Thomas] Jefferson's writing of the Declaration of Independence as a leadership feat. But in reality, Jefferson was a follower when he wrote that document. As the "junior" member of the committee, he was assigned the task by the committee chairs, John Adams and Ben Franklin. Nobody outside of the Continental Congress, except for a few friends, knew that Jefferson had written the Declaration. The fact did not appear in an American newspaper until eight years later in 1784. As a follower, Jefferson lived through all the bell ringing and speechmaking with little public recognition or personal commendation in the press. (Kelley, 1992, p. 48)

Let us examine this particular follower a bit more closely. Perhaps doing so may inspire all of us regarding the impacts we might have, even as followers. Thomas Jefferson was 33 years old when he wrote the Declaration of Independence, having been born April 13, 1743. It would be 25 more years before he became President of the United States. However, the young Jefferson wrote the Declaration of Independence in 17 days, and "it appears he spent most of that time trying to structure into the first two paragraphs at least eight of the 'ancient principles' which he had come to admire" (W. Cleon Skousen, 2007, p. 28). What were those principles?

1) Sound government should be based on self-evident truths; 2) The equal station of mankind here on earth is a cosmic reality, an obvious and inherent aspect of the law of nature and of nature's God; 3) This presupposes (as a self-evident truth) that the Creator made human beings

equal in their rights, before the bar of justice, and equal in His sight; 4) These rights which have been bestowed by the Creator on each individual are unalienable, that is they cannot be taken away or violated without the offender coming under the judgment and wrath of the Creator; 5) Among the most important of the unalienable rights are the right to life, the right to liberty, and the right to pursue whatever course of life a person may desire in search of happiness, so long as it does not invade the inherent rights of others; 6) The most basic reason for a community or a nation to set up a system of government is to assure its inhabitants that the rights of the people shall be protected and preserved; 7) Because this is so, it follows that no office or agency of government has any right to exist except with the consent of the people or their representatives; and 8) If a government either by malfeasance or neglect, fails to protect those rights—or, even worse, if the government itself begins to violate those rights—then it is the right and duty of the people to regain control of their affairs and set up a form of government which will serve the people better. (W. Cleon Skousen, 2007, p. 28)

Not only does the above clearly demonstrate how much influence a follower may have on not just the United States, but as a result, the world's future. It also exhibits the power of—and requirement for—principles which we will examine in the following chapter. "After presenting his work to Benjamin Franklin and John Adams, who made only a few minor changes in the wording, Jefferson submitted the draft to Congress on Friday, June 28, 1776" (Allison, Maxfield, Cook, & Skousen, 2009, p. 68). Suffice it to say, without strong personal principles, Jefferson could never have written those first two paragraphs he apparently spent so much time and energy penning:

When in the Course of human events, it becomes necessary for one people to dissolve the political bands which have connected them with another, and to assume among the powers of the earth, the separate and equal station to which the Laws of Nature and of Nature's God entitle them, a decent respect to the opinions of mankind requires that they should declare the causes which impel them to the separation.

We hold these truths to be self-evident, that all men are created equal, that they are endowed by their Creator with certain unalienable Rights, that among these are Life, Liberty and the pursuit of Happiness. That to secure these rights, Governments are instituted among Men, deriving their just powers from the consent of the governed, that whenever any Form of Government becomes destructive of these ends, it is the Right of the People to alter or to abolish it, and to institute new Government, laying its foundation on such principles and organizing its powers in such form, as to them shall seem most likely to effect their Safety and Happiness. Prudence, indeed, will dictate that Governments long established should not be changed for light and transient causes; and accordingly all experience hath shewn, that mankind are more disposed to suffer, while evils are sufferable, than to right themselves by abolishing the forms to which they are accustomed. But when a long train of abuses and usurpations, pursuing invariably the same Object evinces a design to reduce them under absolute Despotism, it is their right, it is their duty, to throw off such Government, and to provide new Guards for their future security. Such has been the patient sufferance of these Colonies; and such is now the necessity which constrains them to alter their former Systems of Government. The history of the present King of Great Britain is a history of repeated injuries and usurpations, all having in direct object the establishment of an absolute

Tyranny over these States. To prove this, let Facts be submitted to a candid world. (U. S. Declaration of Independence, paragraphs 1-2, 1776)

Notice within the above excerpt, that "government," an organization, "receives its just powers from the consent of the governed." In other words, government receives its power from the followers! Within that Declaration, the followers stated their reasons and rationale for no longer following their leader, and also gave light to their purpose of setting up a new form of government (organization) under new leadership. Today, more than 237 years later, it may still be said of the words of that 33-year-old follower: "While Jefferson was only one among many writers of his time who believed in the principles contained in the Declaration of Independence, surely no one before him or since has expressed those ideas with such inspired force and eloquence" (Allison et al., 2009, p. 71). Jefferson's influence was neither coercive nor manipulative, as we discussed previously, rather, it was inspired and eloquent. To expand on what was mentioned previously, "Thomas Jefferson was not identified as the author of the document until many months later, [in part] due to fear of retaliation by the British" (W. Cleon Skousen, 2007, p. 31). The implication for future followers and leaders is that credit for your efforts may be a long time coming, if at all, even though those efforts may have long-term impact for your organization. When followers can clearly see the source and purpose, marvelous things can happen for the organization. This also opens the door for each follower to become creative, which may lead to innovation.

Seeing Clearly—Key to Creativity

Not only change, but rapid change is something we deal with on an almost daily basis. Some may recall vinyl records as a medium used to play music. They were succeeded by 8-track and cassette tapes, which then gave way to compact discs. Now, we just obtain music over the air, wirelessly, without the necessity for any physical media. These changes occurred over a period of 40 years. During that same period, we've seen advancements in communication that would have seemed impossible not many decades ago. Pew Research reports the following: In January 2014, 90% of American adults had a cellular phone and 58% of American adults had a smartphone; only 64% of Americans had cellular phones in 2002, and 35% of Americans had smart phones in 2011 ("Device ownership over time," 2014)! Among other things, those smart phones consist of a video player, a video camera, a still photo camera, a means of accessing the Internet and a global positioning system. It enables video conferencing and digital voice recording. Without wires or cables, one can communicate next door or around the world in near real-time with just a few keystrokes. It all fits in the palm of your hand at a fraction of the cost those combined devices would demand in the 1990s. Change demands creativity and innovation for your organization as the organization not only learns to apply new technology differently, but also attempts to look ahead to the future for new uses and further development. As with the previous sections, we must clearly see and agree with some basics—this time addressing innovation and creativity.

Innovation may be described as: "The intentional development of a specific product, service, idea, process, or environment for the generation of value" (Oster, 2011, p. 3). On the other hand, "Creativity is a component [of innovation] that enhances the ability of organizations to retain their competitive advantage as well as to stay ahead of their competitors" (Parjanen, 2012, p. 109). "Being creative" implies the ability to ponder about the endless possibilities in a changing world, with something fresh and new. "Creativity is seen by most experts in the field as the process of developing ideas that are both novel and useful" (Burkus, 2014, p. 5). Creativity requires the ability to see clearly what exists now and posture for what may occur in the future. Creativity is "idea generation (ideation)" (Denti & Hemlin, 2012, p. 124007-1) as contrasted to innovation, which is the implementation of ideas. As you may have surmised, prior to become creative, which then has the potential to lead to innovation, it is essential for not only leaders, but followers within the organization to see clearly. This will require removing some rods, just as our initial quotation references.

Creativity is amoral from the standpoint that there may be good or evil purposes underlying the creative event. For example, when you think of the phrase "creative bookkeeping," what comes to mind? You might have imagined some nefarious deed, even though the deed itself may have been creative. Terrorists are continuously creative, such as their heinous act of using passenger airliners as weapons when they struck the United States on September 11, 2001. Also consider young children. They are typically highly creative, which demonstrates that it is an attribute we are all born with to one degree or another. Over time, society or culture provides an environment that either supports or restricts the creativity with which we were born. To regain creativity requires an "intention to be creative and determination to learn and use creative-thinking strategies" (Michalko, 2006, p. xviii). Let's examine this concept a bit more.

Having one's eyes opened with the inherent ability to see in a clear and discerning manner has its roots in the earliest discussions of mankind. We see this in the biblical story of creation:

> God knows that when you eat from it [the tree that is in the middle of the garden, the tree of the knowledge of good and evil] your eyes will be opened...when the woman saw that the fruit of the tree was good for food and pleasing to the eye, and also desirable for gaining wisdom, she took some, and ate it. She also gave some to her husband. (NIV, Gen 3:5-6)

Due to how we have evolved and how paradigms have changed as we have progressed from agrarian to industrial to post-industrial, we need to refocus our eyes and remove rods so that we might see more clearly. "If agriculture is the first stage of economic development and industrialism the second, we can see that still another stage has suddenly been reached" (Toffler, 1971, p. 14). What are those rods and how did they form? If we can agree that we are indeed moving (or have moved) from an industrial to a post-industrial world, let us focus our discussion along that seam.

The emergence of the factory system during the Industrial Revolution posed problems that earlier organizations had not encountered. Work was performed on a much larger scale by a larger number of workers, and required maximum efficiency, leading to hierarchical, bureaucratic organizations (Daft, 2010, p. 23). The factory required standardization from its workforce, not necessarily innovation. On the production line, the essence was moving parts along to complete the task. "This paradigm required size, role clarity, specialization and control. This has given way to speed, flexibility, integration, and innovation" (Ashkenas, Ulruch, Jick, & Kerr, 2002, p. 6) in the post-industrialized world.

The post-industrial age of today has been called many terms. For example, some see it as the age of information. Regardless of the name, "two fundamental forces have shaped the world society: the electronic information revolution and global economic interdependence" (Rosen, Digh, Singer, Philips, & Phillips, 2000, p. 10). These two fundamental forces, can be further subdivided into "technology, travel, trade, and television" (Marquardt & Berger, 2000, p. 3), forming a global interconnectedness, unprecedented in preceding years.

The futurist Samuel Huntington calls our present state "sheer chaos" (Huntington, 1996, p. 35), but not from the standpoint of a lack of order or justice. We see evidence of the chaos of which he speaks as reflective in changes regarding the impacts of nation-states to smaller groupings. Additionally, corporations are increasingly global, expanding beyond national borders. As an example, for decades the United States and the Soviet Union were diametrically opposed with each deterring the other from warfare and potential mutual destruction. Yet, in 2001, a relatively small non-nation-state group known as Al Qaeda launched an attack directly on American soil, and we and other nations around the globe have found ourselves battling against them ever since. "Chaos, complexity, and change are everywhere," (Sanders, 1998, p. 4), not only in the above example. We have already made mention of the changes within the music industry. Within less than one lifetime, recorded music has gone from the reel-to-reel tape, to vinyl records, to 8-tracks, cassettes, MP3 players, CDs and now cloud-based computing. This information age displays intense global competition, rapid and nearly constant change and transformative technological developments, as well as cultural and societal issues.

As we have recently stated, children are, for the most part, born creative, with eyes and their other senses tuned in to their surroundings. Immediately after they are born, they begin to pick up the behaviors and social and cultural traditions the environment offers. Their environment may aid in their creative ability, creating fertile imaginations, or it may detract from their ability to be creative. It seems in our post-industrial world, "our education system is [still] predicated on the idea of academic ability. And there's a reason. The whole system was invented–around the world; there were no public systems of education, really, before the 19th century. They all came into being to meet the needs of industrialism" (Robinson, 2006, p. 3). This may be an aspect that serves to restrict rather than enhance creativity, as young people are molded within, perhaps, an archaic academic system born of an industrial era but serving a post-industrial, information-age world. It may be a condition that unwittingly creates the logs that we've been addressing.

Thus, there needs to be a reinvention of the educational system to facilitate seeing clearly in this new world. Peter Senge, author of the much-heralded book, *The Fifth Discipline* quotes Deming as stating, "we will never transform the prevailing system of management without transforming our prevailing system of education. They are the same system" (p. xiii). "From a very early age we are taught to break apart problems, to fragment the world [and what we are seeing or experiencing]. When we then try to see the big picture we try to reassemble the fragments in our minds" (Senge, 2006, p. 3). Let's see if a metaphor will aid our understanding of the point of the potential ineffectiveness of reassembly in this context. Could a snowstorm be defined by studying the individual flakes? This would be a futile, non-productive effort. We need the ability to see the entire storm to understand what is happening. This would include such things as movement of the storm, winds, and the amount of precipitation—all of which include much more data than what examining a mere flake would provide. Likewise, we could not describe a completed jigsaw puzzle by scrutinizing one piece or even a few pieces grouped together. Others have used the example of blind individuals attempting to clearly see an elephant when feeling singular parts of the elephant's massive frame (e.g., describing the elephant by only being able to feel its trunk). We need an understanding of the complete picture to even have a prayer of putting the entire puzzle together! These essentials are also needed for creativity.

With these reflections stated, the question you are possibly pondering is: "What can I as the leader do?" The following considerations are listed in no particular order of priority. If you have not already found it to be so, leadership is situational. There are no hard and fast rules that will apply to every situation, with the exception of the ethical principles we will discuss in the next chapter. Like the snowstorm example, you and the people in your organization are unique. The environment your organization finds itself to be a part of is also unique. What might work marvelously in one situation may not in another based upon the totality of the elements that define the situation. That really forms the heart of the very first consideration, however, there is another point the leader should continuously remember: "The role of the leader is not to come up with all the great ideas. The role of the leader is to create an environment in which great ideas can happen" (Sinek, 2011, p. 99). The leader enables the creative environment. It is vital for the leader to see that point clearly so that employees have a stake in the outcome, as the Carson example, previously discussed, demonstrated.

Practical Considerations

1) *There are no hard and fast rules*. However, "the responsibility to think and act strategically must become pervasive, not restricted to the C-suite" (Deiser, 2011, p. 18). Each individual, leader, follower, organization and environment is unique. Just as each person has a unique DNA, a similar uniqueness applies for the leader, follower, organization, and environment. Further, ground rules and assumptions may actually limit creativity, creating a barrier. "In tackling a problem, people commonly assume a set of boundaries to limit the solution. Very often the boundaries are imaginary and the solution may lie outside them" (Michalko, 2001, p. 173). How might assumptions fail us (to include leaders), limiting the solution?

On a cold January day, a forty-three-year-old man was sworn in as the chief executive of his country. By his side stood his predecessor, a famous general who, fifteen years earlier, had commanded his nation's armed forces in a war that resulted in the defeat of Germany. The young leader was raised in the Roman Catholic faith. He spent the next five hours watching parades in his honor and stayed up celebrating until three o'clock in the morning (Sinek, 2011, p. 11).

As you read the preceding excerpt from Simon Sinek's book *Start With Why*, your mind may have assumed the subject was President John F. Kennedy. You would be wrong. Until you are made aware that the date being referred to is January 30, 1933, you would never have guessed the above narrative concerns Adolph Hitler. Your assumption would have limited you to discovering the truth, providing an incorrect solution by failing to dig deeper to understand the context of the discussion.

Though written as considerations, leaders are cautioned to take each of these items as points to ponder and adapt them to their situation and circumstances. There is no cookie-cutter approach to leading an organization and applying creative techniques. Wisdom at the individual, leadership and organizational levels impact the creative approach. Having written that, the leader and all members of the organization must resolve to see clearly. "Organizations should never outsource their eyeballs" (Oster, 2011, p. 126) while removing the rods from their eyes. What does that mean? There are two sub-points here. The first is that a holistic, system-view is a good approach. A learning organization is one that includes systems thinking, personal mastery, mental models, shared visions, and team learning, but "systems thinking is the discipline that integrates the [other] disciplines, fusing them together into a coherent body of theory and practice" (Senge, 2006, pp. 11-12). Systems thinking allows us to "see disabilities more clearly—for they are often lost amid the bluster of day-to-day activities" (Senge, 2006, p. 26). As we have learned to view the world and organizations from an industrial age mindset, we must now view them from a holistic system lens, our post-industrial viewpoint, putting pieces back together to examine the entire storm not merely each individual snowflake.

For example, Thomas Edison did not merely bring forward a lamp, but realized "it would require efficient electrical generations, wiring, metered distribution, sockets...all of these separate parts...for one machine" (Utterback, 1996, p. 61). "We live in a world made up of nonlinear dynamical systems" (Sanders, 1998, p. 70), and they need to be viewed in that manner. This is a holistic approach, which takes an innovative vision to a new and larger dimension. The second aspect concerning removing rods relates to eliminating bias while being wisely discerning. "By looking in the mirror and seeing ourselves both as we see ourselves, and as others see us, we have an opportunity to [imagine] powerful new possibilities" (Morgan, 2006, p. 26). We also need an understanding of others: "Leaders who respect others also allow them to be themselves, with creative wants and desires...they approach other people with a sense of their unconditional worth and valuable individual differences" (Northouse, 2010, p. 387). As we will see in subsequent sections, the global environment is one that contains many cultures with varying worldviews. "Culture roots and anchors us" (Rosen et al., 2000, p. 33). As businesses seek to engage on the world stage, they must be attuned to those views, roots, and anchors, or they will fail.

2) *Believe in your creativity*. The primary barriers to believing in your creativity are "fears, uncertainties, and doubts (FUDS). Most people let FUDS control their lives" (Michalko, 2006, p. 3). FUDS could result in individuals, leaders or organizations avoiding creativity by doing the same things as done previously. That will result in stagnation leading to deterioration (as compared to competitors, or as desired by customers) and potential demise of the enterprise. A fear of being wrong could be validated by leadership's zero mistake policy, so it may not be something the followers just imagine. Additionally, if leadership does not provide incentives to creativity, it is pronouncing that creativity is not valued. This leads individuals to not believe in or even make attempts at their own creativity.

A degree of optimism is required to fulfill this consideration. There must be a belief that creativity is possible by the individual, the leader and the members of the organization. "Supportive leadership is positively related to employee creativity" (Parjanen, 2012, p. 112). Creativity must become part of the ethos of the organization where everyone believes they can contribute and make a difference. This will provide the motivation to become creative within the organization's membership, mitigating the effects of FUDS. Why? There will be an atmosphere of safety as it pertains to risk taking. The members will understand that if they take risks and fail, their leadership will use that for learning, not for pruning the ranks. Think of it this way, again recalling what it was like to be a toddler. Rolling over, sitting up, standing upright, walking and eventually running are all risky business (and sometimes humorous) the first time a toddler attempts these activities. Children have uninhibited curiosity and optimism which results in learning and creativity when fears of the inevitable falling down are overcome.

As the organization engages in creative activity, it will experience "collective creativity, not simply the sum of individual creativities but rather intensified and multiplied [creativity]" (Parjanen, 2012, p. 113). Leaders help the organization's members believe that anyone can contribute to the organization's awareness and health. I spoke earlier about Thomas Jefferson, and the fact that, though he was the junior member of the committee, he was assigned to draft the Declaration of Independence. Based upon his leadership's confidence, Jefferson clearly saw what needed to be done and took to the task of drafting that marvelous document. It cannot be emphasized too strongly that within organizations, if everyone is seeing clearly, creativity can occur from any rank within. Once the idea is generated (creativity), the next step, as we mentioned previously, would be to implement the idea through innovation.

3) *Invest time.* A possible barrier to this third consideration is the pressure one might feel to produce, whether that pressure is perceived or actual. It is the drive employees face to achieve whatever metrics the organization's leadership defines. This may result in workers being busy working while at work, or at least appear to be so, without necessarily pausing for reflection. This can lead to overcrowded schedules with no time to contemplate new approaches. Again, this could result in following tried and true techniques without actually thinking about alternatives and generating new and fresh ideas. They would fail to become creative. Being creative takes time, so allowances within the operating environment should be established just to ponder...to collaborate...to create! While pondering, fleeting ideas may come to mind and they should be written down rather than relying on memory. It may also require that the individual or group puts the problem or issue aside and returns to it at a later time. This is likened to remembering a person's name some time <u>after</u> you stopped trying to remember that name.

At this point, you might wonder, "How much time should be spent?" The answer: whatever it takes, with the understanding that your organization exists to perform in the here and now, in addition to the then. This means there must be a balance. One technique to generate ideas is to give yourself an idea quota. We will see this employed shortly, but for now, "a quota and time limit focus your energy in a way that guarantees profluency [sic] of thought...allowing us to generate more imaginative alternatives than we otherwise would" (Michalko, 2001, p. 90). Again we ask, "How much time should CEOs invest?" "CEOs who are deeply committed to growth devote 20% to 40% of their time to these activities" (Laurie & Harreld, 2013, p. 3). CEOs are not the only ones who need to invest the time. Time should also be carved out for employee training. That is an area that inspires seeing clearly as it demonstrates the desire for everyone to take responsibility and become involved.

It also combats whatever negative effects arose from the educational system, as previously mentioned. "When you share responsibility with [leadership training] teams, it really gets people thinking about ownership" (Marquardt & Berger, 2000, p. 88). As the teams are trained, and as they take on ownership, conditions are ripe for creativity. Remember, "under the right conditions, everyone can generate great ideas" (Burkus, 2014, p. 11). It just may take a bit of time, so leadership must have patience. Moreover, it is not necessarily experts who will provide those fresh ideas, as they may have rods in their own eyes. "People who solve tough problems often come from the edge of a domain. They have enough knowledge to understand the problem, but don't have a fixed method of thinking" (Burkus, 2014, p. 85). This avoids "what [Harvard's Chris] Argyris calls skilled incompetence—teams full of people who are incredibly proficient at keeping themselves from learning" (Senge, 2006, p. 25). These are people who seem to have a vested interest in maintaining the status quo, and, perhaps, their level of comfort, which runs counter to growth and learning, creativity and innovation.

4) *Be a diversity enabler.* Leaders must enable groups within their organizations to work laterally or cross-functionally to enhance their creativity. We will address this more fully in later chapters, but suffice it to say, "many achievements in companies involve collaboration between creative individuals, each with varying knowledge, skills, life experience, perspectives, and expertise, [with the ability to] tackle multi-faceted challenges that cannot be met individually" (Parjanen, 2012, pp. 109-110). Beware of those individuals who are stuck in the status-quo mode of thinking. They will be ready to stifle or attack change ideas, perhaps resulting in ideas being killed or seriously wounded in the earliest stages of development, wittingly or unwittingly sabotaging the gains that could have been made. "If problems are solved the way they always have been solved, it blocks creativity and prevents new ideas from penetrating" (Parjanen, 2012, p. 111).

Additionally, the organization may be set up in a stove-piped fashion where the various sub-groups have little to no contact with other sub-groups. This has the effect of limiting the holistic approach essential for idea creation. Diversity should be "sought across boundaries, and at all levels, [with the] call for a new culture of leadership that shapes horizontal, non-hierarchical relationships without relying on formal power and control" (Deiser, 2011, p. 18). For example, it was Lewis Howard Latimer, Thomas Edison's employee, "who invented a process to make carbon filaments that made electric lights affordable" (Watts, 2014), allowing Edison's light bulb to function for more than a few days.

Of course, before looking at others within the organization, you should examine yourself for any rods impacting your ability to see clearly and preventing your ability for diverse thought. Varying one's perspective is a practical approach to seeing clearly, by "restating a problem many different ways, and diagramming, mapping and drawing a problem" (Michalko, 2001, p. 17). This concurs with the fifth of Covey's Seven Habits: "Seek first to understand then to be understood" (Covey, 1989, p. 235). The leader is not only responsible to himself for seeing clearly, but he must also help others to do likewise, providing them with the same sight picture. This sight picture "must make sense to others [and] must be understandable" (Handy, 1989, pp. 134-135).

5) *Initially proactively strive for quantity over quality.* When reaching for ideas to begin the creativity process, resist the urge to evaluate the quality of the idea. The goal is to generate as many ideas as time will permit, without qualifications or restrictions, and also to accept them all without eliminating any. Hand in hand with a lack of diversity, "if you look at a problem from the same perspective as you have always done, you're going to come up with the same old answers and roadblocks" (Buggie, 1982, p. 69). So you must alter your perspective.

Having a diverse group where the same problem can be approached from multiple vantage points will also provide variety in perspective. Again, thinking about young children, they sometimes annoyingly continue to ask "Why?" "Perceiving your problem from different levels of abstraction changes the implications of the problem...asking "Why" four or five times [helps to] find the level where you are comfortable" (Michalko, 2001, p. 25). While relearning creativity, seek that childlike essence of discovery, remembering, "from the moment we are born, we spend almost every waking hour working to fit in with our family, playmates, classmates, teachers, colleagues, and fellow churchgoers" (Oster, 2011, p. 236). This, "trying to fit," could actually limit the creative juices that might otherwise flow forth. Proactivity will be required. It "comes from seeing how we contribute to our own problems...all too often proactiveness is reactiveness in disguise" (Senge, 2006, p. 21).

One scholar relates the story of a Japanese fishing villager who, unlike his neighbors, built his home facing the direction of perennial tsunamis. Though his neighbors' homes faced away from the direction of those tsunamis, this villager was able to see clearly what was going on in the surrounding environment, noting various weather phenomena as it approached in real time and, by proactively acting upon true knowledge, he was able to take steps to survive the next event. "He could not take control of the sea but he managed his responses to it in the most effective ways" (Gryskiewicz, 1999, p. xix). There is no time in this environment for head-in-the-sand methodologies as evidenced by the fishing villager's neighbors.

Thomas Edison and other well-known creative personalities fully embraced this concept of productivity and quantity: "Edison held 1,093 patents…guaranteed productivity by giving himself a personal quota of one minor invention every ten days and a major invention every six months…Bach wrote a cantata every week, even when sick…Einstein is best known for his paper on relativity, but he published 248 other papers" (Michalko, 2001, p. 10). So, as we conclude this consideration, remember: "More bad poems were composed by the major poets than the minor poets. They composed more bad poems than minor poets because they produced more poetry" (Michalko, 2001, p. 85). It took Edison "nine thousand experiments to perfect the light bulb" (Michalko, 2001, p. 85), and he is quoted as saying, "I didn't find a way to make a lightbulb [sic], I found a thousand ways how not to make one" (Sinek, 2011, p. 101). So if you want to have a breakthrough idea, proactively seek a high quantity of ideas to dramatically increase your odds!

Chapter Summary

- A leader's values yield his or her beliefs, which result in the leader's behavior. This behavior is evidence to followers of what that leader believes and values.
- Seeing clearly (SC) is not only a leader's responsibility, but it is also the obligation of the entire organization.
- Distraction and lack of discernment limit one's ability to see clearly.
- Leading is a relationship process between people, whereby a person (or group) influences others to achieve a mutually agreed upon goal, mission or purpose.
- Creativity is intentional and determined idea generation as contrasted with innovation, which is the implementation of creativity.
- A holistic, system-view provides a perspective the myopic, close-in view will not.
- The leader enables the creative environment within the organization, and does not have to be the sole creative force.

Questions to Ponder

1. What presently may be hampering your ability to see clearly? What are the logs or rods that may be blocking your view?
2. When was the last time you thought about why you are doing whatever it is that you do? If you have never done so, do it now and think about what you discovered.
3. Do you participate in an organization where you are an assigned or emergent leader or both? Give instances of each.
4. Do you participate in an organization where you are in a followership role? Provide instances of any followership role you perceive.
5. Do you believe that you can be creative? Why or why not?
6. In the past, have you considered yourself to be a leader? How do you feel about that now?
7. Who do you influence and how? Who influenced you and how did they accomplish that?

Chapter 2

PRINCIPLES - THE FOUNDATION

"Love the Lord your God with all your heart, with all your soul, and with all your mind ... "
(Matthew 22:37)

"But America, as I look at you from afar, I wonder whether your moral and spiritual progress has been commensurate with your scientific progress (King, 1958). This was a question Dr. Martin Luther King, Jr. posed to listeners in various fora, one being the inaugural convention of the newly established United Presbyterian Church, U.S.A. Could not the question of morals, spiritual progress, and ethical principles apply equally today, not just in the United States, but also globally?

There are many types of principles: principles of biochemistry, of magnetism, of crop improvement, of golf. Principles are "a governing law of conduct; an opinion, attitude, or belief that exercises a directing influence on the life and behavior; a rule or code of usually good conduct by which one directs one's life or actions" ("Principle," 2014). For the purpose of this discussion, however, we are concerned with ethical principles, as this is the centerpiece of being able to see clearly.

As we will discuss shortly, let us establish values as "shared goals, beliefs, ideals, and purposes" (Kuczmarski & Kuczmarski, 1995, p. 25), and, therefore, are formed by the individual or organization, based upon principles. Virtues, on the other hand, are "rooted in the heart of the individual, and are not innate but can be acquired and learned through practice. People can be taught by their families and communities to be morally appropriate human beings" (Northouse, 2010, p. 381). We can be taught to not only see this clearly, but also have a commensurate moral and spiritual progression! By ethics, we mean "the discipline dealing with what is good and bad or right and wrong or with moral duty and obligation" ("Ethics," 2014), which is similar to the definition of morals: "of or relating to principles or considerations of right and wrong action or good and back character" ("Moral," 2014). We see with these definitions that there must be some means or method of assessing what is good, bad, right or wrong. Mankind has wrestled with this particular issue—that being the source for understanding what is good, bad, right, or wrong—throughout the ages. "Ethics does not describe what is good for me in the sense of my own happiness, but what is good for me in the sense of my honest understanding of the good, of my being captivated by values. In the one case, I myself am...the standard of my judgement [sic]; in the other, the standard...lies outside myself." (Joas, 2000, p. 183). A premise of this work is that values, ethics and morals, which inform our principles, indeed emanate from outside ourselves, and that singular source is God. This will be expanded upon shortly.

Sadly, the problem stated by Dr. King concerning our lack of moral and spiritual progress surrounds us. His point was well taken. Today, we can marvel at our technological advances, but have we advanced morally? This question becomes virtually bone chilling, as demonstrations of the lack of moral and spiritual progress seem to occur with an alarming frequency and in all manners of leadership venues. How does it happen? All too often, "leadership induces and maintains a leader's belief that he is somehow excepted from moral requirements that apply to the rest of us" (Ciulla, 2004, p. 138). These leaders fail to see that they are indeed not excepted from ethical matters. For example, so-called rebels in Libya, aided by North Atlantic Treaty Organization (NATO) forces, brutally killed their 42-year despot leader, Muammar Gaddafi. The Prime Minister of Greece and the Prime Minister of Italy both abandoned their posts within days of each other, while surrounded by intrigue and duplicitous behavior. Pennsylvania State University's fifteen-year head football coach, Joseph Paterno, was fired due to his alleged failure to lead concerning his lack of action regarding his assistant coach's sexual abuse charges. "Washington, D.C. mayor Marion Barry's cocaine habit and late-night hotel rendezvousing ended in a sting operation, jail sentence, and international disgrace for the Capitol City" (Chaleff, 2009, p. 114). Each of these leadership failures received nationwide, if not global, attention. They exemplify leadership fiascos due to ethical failures. These leaders seemed to believe they were exempt from the morals that other citizens face, forgetting that, as Winston Churchill stated, "The higher up the ape climbs the more you see of his behind" (Zweifel, 2003, p. i), as a metaphor for the increasing ease with which flaws are observed as one climbs the corporate or societal ladder. Organizations bear the brunt of failed ethical leadership, as we think of the above organizations, the 2001 Enron scandal, or the situation surrounding a London bank:

What several European revolutions, two world wars and numerous depressions could not do to London's Barings Bank in more than 200 years, one 28-year-old employee accomplished with a few computer keystrokes. And the bank collapsed...management was alerted months ago to the inadequacies of its oversight systems. But management chose to ignore that advice, presumably because everyone seemed to benefit from the system as it was. (Mendonca, 2001, pp. 266-267)

Failed ethical leadership, reflecting a lack of the principles leadership should seek, is not solely a 21st century phenomena. Recall the story of King David as written in 2 Samuel 11:2-5:

One evening David got up from his bed and strolled around on the roof of the palace. From the roof he saw a woman bathing —a very beautiful woman. So David sent someone to inquire about her, and he reported, 'This is Bathsheba, daughter of Eliam and wife of Uriah the Hittite.' David sent messengers to get her, and when she came to him, he slept with her. Now she had just been purifying herself from her uncleanness. Afterward, she returned home. The woman conceived and sent word to inform David: 'I am pregnant.' (*HCSB Study Bible, Holman Christian Standard Bible: God's word for life*, 2010)

That story concludes with David sending Bathsheba's husband, Uriah, out to the very forward of the front lines of the fiercest battle, where, as David had planned, Uriah perished. Having her husband killed so he might have that man's wife is clearly failed ethical leadership on the part of King David. The ethical leadership dilemma is, therefore, not a new phenomenon in today's world. What is different for leaders is the dynamic of the organizations themselves, due to rapid increases in information technology, the changing nature of the work force and the resulting potential for global impact due to proper or improper decisions. This is the moral and spiritual progress Dr. King found lacking.

Within the past decade, a Nigerian scholar posed the leadership issues within his country as follows: "To win the war on corruption, adherence to ethical standards in decision-making must be the foundation of the nation's policies. Individuals can deliberately shape their characters to be virtuous" (Lanre-Abass, 2008, p. 137). For this work, we use the umbrella term, "principles," as we explore ethics, character, values and virtue. We also note that the Nigerian scholar states what this paper believes, that you and I can deliberately shape our characters to be virtuous…if only we could clearly see what being virtuous means! That is what we hope to gain from this chapter. One thing is certain, whether one is a leader or a follower, there will be challenges to deal with, and "crisis judges the condition of our character [which] comes out under fire" (Guinnes et al., 2000, p. 79). Therefore, it is important to consider the source of our principles now, during the calm periods.

Consider the Source

As you think about the principles that guide you, have you considered what your source is for those principles? Is it just handed down from parent to child, or some authority such as government? We should take time to reflect on those questions, as they are fundamental to our ability to lead. Remember, we want to remove the logs from our own eyes, so that we might see clearly. So, first we must deal with ourselves.

After Jesus' resurrection, as a prelude to The Great Commission, He presented to His disciples and said, "All authority has been given to Me in heaven and on earth" (Matthew 28:18, HCSB). Jesus' use of the word "all" should be noted and regarded with care by earthly leaders. Not some, not most, but <u>all</u> authority. This has implications for leaders past, present and future. It has implications for our discussion. We must begin here, because leaders must "understand [see clearly] that what we believe precedes policy and practice" (DePree, 2004, p. 26). This is why we view principles as the first of the three main elements of SC, because what we believe is rooted in our principles, which precedes everything we say and do.

Moreover, as Winston (2002) notes, "leadership starts with values" (p. 1). We touched on an ethics definition earlier, but another scholar defines ethics as being "about how we distinguish between right and wrong, or good and evil in relation to the actions, volitions, and character of human beings" (Ciulla, 2004, p. xv). The leader's values will, therefore, have a direct bearing on how he or she relates to the people in the organization as well as the organization's purpose. So, the sage leader should concern himself with determining the source of those values.

This issue, that of the <u>source</u> of values, is foundational to the leadership this paper professes, hence, this early discussion, and emphasis, of its merits. As it bears repeating, we need to understand (see clearly) that human leaders are not the source of values—God is. Let us dwell on this for a moment. C.S. Lewis, the author of *Mere Christianity*, wrote: "If the Moral Law was one of our instincts, we ought to be able to point to some one impulse inside us which was always what we call 'good,' always in agreement with the rule of right behaviour. But you cannot" (Lewis, 1980, p. 11). Let's look at a brief example to further highlight this point.

Let us suppose you are walking near a pool and hear a man who is in the water cry out. There may be an impulse within you to dive into the water to help. Conversely, there may be another impulse to ignore the man and go about your merry way. What is it within you that helps you determine which action to take? There must be some overriding authority that supersedes those impulses. There must be something that triggers a sense of disgust, when proper action is not taken. Let us turn from the hypothetical to reality. As you review, you will undoubtedly have a sense or a general understanding of what the proper action should have been:

Twenty-eight-year-old Catherine Genovese, who was called Kitty by almost everyone in the neighborhood, was returning home from her job as manager of a bar in Hollis. She parked her red Fiat in a lot adjacent to the Kew Gardens Long Island Railroad Station, facing Mowbray Place. Like many residents of the neighborhood, she had parked there day after day since her arrival from Connecticut a year ago, although the railroad frowns on the practice. For more than half an hour 38 respectable, law-abiding citizens in Queens watched a killer stalk and stab her in three separate attacks in Kew Gardens. Twice [the citizens'] chatter and the sudden glow of their bedroom lights interrupted him and frightened him off. Each time he returned, sought her out, and stabbed her again. Not one person telephoned the police during the assault; one witness called after the woman [Kitty] was dead. (Gansberg, 1964, p. 27)

As you read the preceding text, is there not something that swells up inside of you telling you that the inaction of those neighbors was wrong? So again, if moral law or values do not originate from ourselves, or, in the context of leadership, from the organization's leader, then where do they come from? Jesus expressed foundational values in the Beatitudes, found in Matthew 5:3-9 (Winston, 2002, p. iv). These foundational values and their meanings are displayed in Table 1.

Table 1. Foundational Values in Beatitudes

Bible Verse	Foundational Value	Meaning
Matthew 5:3	Poor in spirit	Humble
Matthew 5:4	Mourn	Care for others
Matthew 5:5	Meek	Controlled discipline—being angry at the right occasion, with right people, for right length of time
Matthew 5:6	Hunger and thirst for righteousness	Seek what is right, good, just, equitable
Matthew 5:7	Merciful	Forgiveness, compassion
Matthew 5:8	Pure in heart	Integrity and focused purpose
Matthew 5:9	Peacemakers	Make and keep peace

[Adapted from: Winston, B. E. (2002). *Be a leader for God's sake--From values to behaviors*]

Further, Winston (2002) purports the above foundational values are all based upon *agapao* love, "moral love, doing the right thing at the right time for the right reason...more specifically to love in a social or moral sense" (p. 5). Stated alternatively, "the most crucial objective for any leader is personal growth" (Blackaby & Blackaby, 2011, p. 51). Did you catch that? *Your personal growth is key to your leadership.* Again, this tracks with our premise that you must first remove the logs in your own eyes before you can see clearly to remove dust from your neighbor's (meaning co-worker, subordinate, supervisor, etc.) eyes. It also implies that learning is involved as growth occurs. Where you chose to receive your personal growth is, therefore, key to how your leadership will develop. This is why we emphasize that the root of values is found in God and in no other place. The *agapao* love is an *active* love, and is summarized as follows:

> *Love is patient, love is kind.*
> *Love does not envy,*
> *is not boastful, is not conceited,*
> *does not act improperly,*
> *is not selfish, is not provoked,*
> *and does not keep a record of wrongs.*
> *Love finds no joy in unrighteousness*
> *but rejoices in the truth.*
> *It bears all things, believes all things,*
> *hopes all things, endures all things.*
> *Love never ends.*
> (1 Corinthians 13: 4-8, HCSB)

How well you see the above will affect how you live your life and how you interact with those in your home, school, church, and work environment. It is well worth the time to reflect so as to clearly see where the source of the principles that guide your words and actions resides. Perhaps now is the time to do so.

Principles can Bloom—"Weeds" Must be Removed

Imagine that you are living alone on a deserted island. You have the wherewithal to make your own shelter and sustain yourself with food. As the hours turn to days, and the days to weeks then months, perhaps you might have a sense of loneliness, but there would be no relationship for you to nurture. You might find yourself communing with the animals on that island. You would probably be desperate for some human contact. However, the months slip into years, as you realize that you are alone. Would there be ethical considerations in that sort of environment?

Though the previous section concerned our *internal* nature, ethics and values, like leadership, are about relationships, the *interaction* between persons. The obvious implication is that communication (interaction) and ethical considerations require more than one person. "The study of ethics has to do with developing standards for judging the conduct of one party whose behavior affects another" (Ciulla, 2004, p. 28). Samuel Adams, one of America's Founding Fathers, wrote: "...neither the wisest constitution nor the wisest laws will secure the liberty and happiness of a people whose manners are universally corrupt...will not suffer a man to be chosen into any office of power and trust who is not a wise and virtuous man" (Skousen, 2006, p. 59). Ethics is not about a constitution or laws, but concerns people whose manners are not universally corrupt. This corruption is what we mean when we write about *weeds*. These weeds are those elements of our being that usher forth a lack of virtue or moral values. Regarding leadership and leaders, "ethics has to do with what leaders do and who leaders are" (Northouse, 2010, p. 378). To further drive home this point, the second President of the United States, John Adams, is quoted as saying: "Our Constitution was made only for a moral and religious people. It is wholly inadequate to the government of any other" (Carson, 2012, p. 133). Combined, these admonitions bring us to an offshoot of ethical and virtuous leadership, that of trust.

"From the perspective of Western tradition, the development of ethical theory dates back to Plato (427-347 B. C.) and Aristotle (384-322 B. C.). Ethical theories can be thought of as falling within two broad domains: theories about leaders' *conduct* and theories about leaders' *character*" (Northouse, 2010, p. 378). Pursuit of a conduct approach would entail examination of rules or consequences of the leader's actions. Though both are important when examining leadership attributes, we have been exploring character, that is, who leaders are as people as we've explored virtue as a leadership attribute. Moreover, we have already made the case, that a person's character will be reflected by their actions, by their conduct. However, we recognize that "leaders are not born virtuous; they become virtuous through training and experience" (Galston, 2010, p. 101), and we understand the source of values and morals. Even as we examine the founding of the Unites States of America as a governmental body—a large organization—scholars have observed, "a free people cannot survive under a republican [meaning self-government, not the political party] constitution unless they remain virtuous and morally strong" (Skousen, 2006, p. 49).

Being accountable, transparent, communicative and humble enhances trust, but the roots of all those qualities are the values and ethics, the central principles upon which trust is built. Though values and ethics do not originate with the leader, the leader sets the organization's environment as she forms a relationship with her employees. "To achieve ethical behavior an entire organization, from top to bottom, must make a commitment to it, the model for that commitment has to originate from the top" (Ciulla, 2004, p. 41). We saw this aspect of commitment previously as we reviewed Ben Carson and his relationship with his mother. It means not only must leaders walk the talk, they must also talk the walk.

This trusting environment, established by the leader, will encourage growth-essential risk-taking by employees. "If frontline employees are actually to make decisions that entail some risk, they must have a sense of security. They must know that they are allowed to make mistakes" (Carlzon, 1989, p. 83). Additionally, "employees who trust their executives, managers, and supervisors are more likely to report misconduct" (Plinio, Young, & Lavery, 2010, p. 195). "The values and ethically focused organization would clearly see wrong decisions being used as the basis for training and right decisions being used as opportunities for praise and reinforcement" (Carlzon, 1989, p. 83). Listen to how one leader expresses her reaction to poor behavior or performance:

It's never easy or pleasant. But after dealing with it [poor performance], if the person is still part of our team, I watch him or her closely so that as soon as possible, I can catch that person doing something right. I prefer praising and celebrating successes to dealing with problems. (Blanchard & Barrett, 2011, p. 12)

Notice from the above text, this leader watches the poor performer closely to "catch them doing something right" so as to offer praise! How often would the opposite technique be undertaken, seeking to ascertain when the poor performer was doing something else wrong so as to punish? Imagine the trust that would ensue from the former as an approach instead of the latter.

We might even consider examining this aspect from the standpoint of desiring the employee to take ownership of the organization's values. To do that, there must be trust in the leadership, and to have that trust, leaders must demonstrate integrity. Stated alternatively, "Trust is fed by personal integrity. Trust grows when we keep our promises and follow through on our commitments" (Freiberg & Freiberg, 1997, p. 109). Let's briefly look at an example. During contract negotiations with union workers, then Southwest Airlines CEO Herb Kellerher told Gary Kerans, union president, that if the contract went through, he would freeze his own salary and bonus for five years. Apparently, what's good for Southwest's pilots is good for its chairman as well" (Freiberg & Freiberg, 1997, p. 110). This is an example of walking the talk and is sure to encourage trust.

We began this section musing about living on a totally deserted island. The deserted island idea is indeed fictitious because we certainly do not live in isolation, but as we have stated, we live with relationships. However, over time, mankind's environment has changed from agrarian to industrial, to what Clawson calls a "new infocracy" (Clawson, 2000, p. 76). We have seen the agrarian society's leadership model as mainly aristocratic, "conferred leadership and power by birthright…the Industrial Revolution changed that…dukes and earls were ill prepared to administer the then new emerging bureaucracies" (Clawson, 2000, p. 77). During that period, we see the rise of people like Carnegie, Rockefeller, Ford, Jobs, Gates, and Trump, to name a few, whose personalities are etched on their companies. Some postulate that the current information age shifts decision making to lower levels—the levels where information resides. Even so, this changing environment does not alleviate the leader of the responsibility for ethical leadership. On the contrary, it makes the situation much more complicated due to the speeding up of the discover process of any misbehavior on the part of those leaders. "Today's leaders face tremendous pressure from government and the public to hold their organizations and employees to high ethical and professional standards" (Daft, 2010, p. 8). In an instant, pictures taken using seemingly ever-present cell phones can document any inappropriate event, and can then be forwarded to many people in seconds. So, leaders are under scrutiny as never before, and barely a month transpires without the global exposure of failed principles, whether in the corporate world, or in government or even in the church. We do, however, have positive role models.

Let us examine what has been written about Dag Hammarskjöld, the second Secretary-General of the United Nations. He served in that position from April 1953 until September 1961. While considering whether personal value systems influence leadership agendas, managerial styles, and organizational culture, we read:

Regardless of whether an administrator blatantly reveals a particular ethical framework or moral persuasion, these personal components are instrumental and interactive with the organization's operational culture. Service and self-sacrifice were the first stratum of his ethical code…He [Hammarskjöld] died in a plane crash during a peace mission in the Republic of Congo while attempting to negotiate a cease-fire between Congo forces and non-combatant United Nations forces. Among the documents found with his body were copies of the United Nations Charter, the New Testament, and the Book of Psalms. (Lyon, 2007, p. 84)

As we read this brief account, we see aspects of the Beatitudes we addressed previously (e.g., care for others, self-sacrifice, pure in heart, peacemaker). We get the sense that Hammarskjöld was a man of humility as well. One of the verses "Hammarskjöld cited was Psalms 37:7–8, Hold thee still in the Lord…fret not thyself, else shalt thou be moved to evil" (Lyon, 2007, p. 88). With this vignette we observe a man who knew the origin of the principles he held dear, and that it is indeed possible in our world to embody the virtuous character with humility. It has been said, "people with humility don't think less of themselves; they just think of themselves less" (Blanchard & Barrett, 2011, p. 114). However, ethical behavior is not without its challenges or barriers.

As we consider the relational aspect of ethical behavior, we can also observe that there are barriers to ethical behavior—weeds—which may be viewed from both top-down and bottom-up perspectives. By top-down we mean the pressure emanates from the senior leader to the subordinates. Conversely, bottom-up means the pressure radiates from the subordinates, often to the point of it becoming standard practice. They are rationalizations subordinates may use to act in an unprincipled manner.

Four typically top-down pressures that impede the ethical process are: "1) performance is what counts in the end; 2) by all means show that you are loyal and a team player; 3) do not break the law; and 4) do not over-invest in ethical behavior" (Mihelic, Lipicnik, & Tekavcic, 2010, p. 34). If performance is what counts in the end, then perhaps shortcuts may be attempted, some of which might stretch the bounds of ethical behavior. There must be continuous demonstration of the right behavior for followers to perceive that the boss is ethical. In conjunction with the words the leader choses, their actions speak volumes about their character and the cultural environment they will foster. The leader may view being told, "he or she doesn't have any clothes on," as being disloyal even if it is truthful. These pressures silence the development of good ideas due to fear. The leader must encourage truthful feedback and demonstrate principled, ethical behavior.

Four rationalizations, which are typically bottom-up, include: "1) it's standard practice, everyone in the company does this on a regular basis; 2) it's not a big deal (a lukewarm form of apology); 3) it's not my responsibility; and 4) I want to be loyal" (Mihelic et al., 2010, p. 34). These rationalizations are employed because sometimes it's easier to use them than it is to stand up for what is right, principled, and ethical. It is for this reason it is imperative that the leader fosters an ethical environment that encourages honest and open dialogue. With those as challenges, how might a leader determine if an ethical climate is being promoted within the organization or if there are issues lying beneath the surface? Does the leader:

- Set an example of ethical behavior by his or her own actions?
- Facilitate the development and dissemination of a code of ethical conduct?
- Initiate discussions with followers or colleagues about ethics and integrity?
- Recognize and reward ethical behavior by others?
- Take personal risks to advocate moral solutions to problems?
- Help others find fair and ethical solutions to conflicts?
- Initiate support services (e.g. ethics hotline, on-line advisory group)? (Yukl, 2010, p. 430)

So, an approach to increase ethical behavior is for individual leaders (and followers) to encourage ethical practices and oppose unethical activities or decisions. Supporting this approach could be a technique where organizational programs are used to help individuals develop positive values, increase awareness of ethical issues, encourage ethical behavior, and discourage unethical practices (Yukl, 2010, p. 430). Regardless of approach, the essence remains, that the source of ethics and values is God. This must be seen very clearly by the leader and by extension, the organization, to include national organizations.

From a global government perspective, several nations have indicated they see clearly the need for ethical behavior. Since December 14, 1960, 34 countries have signed the Convention on the Organisation for Economic Co-operation and Development (OECD). These nations include: Australia, Austria, Belgium, Canada, Chile, Czech Republic, Denmark, Estonia, Finland, France, Germany, Greece, Hungary, Iceland, Ireland, Israel, Italy, Japan, Korea, Luxembourg, Mexico, Netherlands, New Zealand, Norway, Poland, Portugal, Slovak Republic, Slovenia, Spain, Sweden, Switzerland, Turkey, United Kingdom and the United States. OECD's mission is "to promote policies that will improve the economic and social well-being of people around the world" ("List of OECD Member countries - Ratification of the Convention on the OECD," n.d.). The following are some of the fundamental points the member nations agreed to regarding ethics, values and principles:

1. Core values underpin public service. Identifying core values is the first step to creating a common understanding within society of the expected behaviour of public office holders;
2. Putting values into effect starts with communication. Use training to raise awareness of public servants on ethical issues;
3. Ensure integrity in daily management;
4. Monitor compliance; and
5. Taking action against wrongdoing as a shared responsibility of managers and external investigative bodies. ("Building public trust: Ethics measures in OECD countries," 2000)

As the list above indicates, core values are essential. These nations recognize this fact because they understand the relationship nature of our existence on this planet and in the global community. If nations can see this clearly, what does it bode for smaller organizations down to the individual level?

Practical Considerations

1) *Be a good observer.* Covey wrote "seek first to understand, then to be understood" (Covey, 1991, p. 235). Leaders should like people. Jesus stated in Matthew 19:19, "love your neighbor as you do yourself." To the maximum extent practical, the principled leader actively demonstrates interest in his followers. By opening up to followers, while exhibiting high standards of ethical behavior, the follower will understand that the principles the leader purports are more than just words; they are indeed part of the organization's culture beginning at the leadership level.

2) *Ask tough questions.* Ethical issues are not necessarily visible or obvious. "One might consider corporate culture as an iceberg. Above the surface might include symbols, ceremonies, stories, dress and physical settings, but below surface includes values, assumptions, beliefs, attitudes and feelings" (Daft, 2010, p. 375). The leader will probably need to engage with subordinates while asking questions to dig into those issues below the surface. Like the iceberg, the greatest issues may be those that are below the surface, unseen until disaster strikes. We will revisit this as we discuss culture in more detail.

3) *Understand what is core.* How does the situation relate to the company's overall strategy? Are the standards the highest possible? Are people being put first (or is leadership self-serving)? Businesses must be profitable, but the principled leader asks whether profit is an end to itself. What is the purpose of the organization? Remember, it is for that purpose that the leader and follower are joined into an organization. These three considerations will be further developed as we discuss people and purpose. However, scholars concur on the following four essential values for ethical leaders, greatly similar to the aforementioned Beatitudes:

- *Pride.* This is not meant to be self-love. Psalm 139:14 provides context: "I will praise You because I have been remarkably and wonderfully made." This value is about having a healthy pride, not vanity. If the ethical leader does not possess self-esteem, she can hardly expect esteem or respect from her followers
- *Patience.* As leaders work toward the realization of their vision (to include enacting organizational change), there will undoubtedly be resistance or obstacles, both internal and external to the organization. Time (and effort) will be required to overcome those obstacles, necessitating patience. Patience takes only moments to destroy, but years to build up against the obstacles.
- *Persistence.* Within the Bible, 2 Timothy 4:7 provides a great verse to remind the ethical leader of what is required with respect to persistence: "I have fought the good fight, I have finished the race, I have kept the faith." The ethical leader does not let impediments weaken his resolve to finish the race, to stay the course. The ethical leader takes the necessary steps to achieve the clearly seen vision, even if those steps involve personal sacrifice and risk.
- *Perspective.* The leader being able to reflect on the situation at hand enables this value. "Reflection is simply not possible unless one devotes some time each day to silence, a resource that has been recommended by the wisest of all time and yet the one resource that remains most untapped. It is the inner silence that allows one to reflect on the higher purpose, to question one's decisions in light of that purpose, and to seek the strength not to betray it" (Mendonca, 2001, p. 274). We will explore this aspect of a respite further on, but having come this far, why not take a moment or two and capture that silence, and reflect on the many tasks you face?

The leader not only exists in a relationship with her organization. She and the organization exist in a relationship with the global environment. We will discuss that environment and relationship in following chapters, but as alluded to previously, organizations of today are much more connected with each other than ever before. This connectivity provides opportunities for new relationships as well as challenges. The principled leader sees clearly both the internal and external environment, and understands relationship building within those domains while remaining principled in dealing with both.

Chapter Summary

- Values, ethics and morals, which inform our principles, emanate from outside ourselves, and that singular source is God.
- Barriers to ethical behavior can be formed from both top-down and bottom-up perspectives.
- Pride, patience, persistence and perspective as core values can be used to enhance one's ethical behavior.

Questions to Ponder

1. From where do you see your source of ethics, values, and principles originating?
2. Is love a foundational value for how you lead; for how you follow? Why or why not?
3. How would you want the world (family, job, friends) to view you?
4. Have you considered closely monitoring a poor performer while looking for the good in what they are doing so as to encourage them?
5. Are you tired of being praised at work or at home? Do you practice patience with others?
6. Does your organization tolerate people who do not live up to the organization's values? How is that situation handled?

Chapter 3

PEOPLE – HIRED HEARTS

"Love your neighbor as yourself"
(Matthew 22:39)

Since leadership is a "process of influencing others," questions one might ask are: "*How* does one influence others?" "*What* is the process or media through which influence occurs?" and "*Why* would one accept influencing attempts?" To answer these questions, we must dig deeper into the relationship the leader has with the follower, and the follower with the leader, by examining culture and communication. Fundamental to this discussion is trust between the communicating parties. Following this discussion, we will see more clearly the necessity of a trusting relationship, remembering again that *the purpose of the organization is to do something.*

Two biblical verses succinctly express the notion of considering followers as "hired hearts." The first occurs during the creation event where we are told: "The LORD God said, 'It is not good for the man to be alone. I will make a helper suitable for him'" (Genesis 2:18, NIV). By making a helper, the first human organization was created. That organization consisted of one man and one woman, created and joined by the power of God Himself. Secondly, it is repeated no less than nine times within the New Testament, "Love your neighbor as yourself" (Matthew 5:43, 19:19, 22:39; Mark 12:31, 12:33; Luke 10:27; Romans 13:9; Galatians 5:14; and James 2:8).

To examine the concept of "loving one's neighbor as yourself," let us begin with an understanding of the word *love* in this context. The love that is being referred to here has been described as "*agapao* love, the love of a friend, doing the right thing at the right time for the right reason" (Winston, 2009, p. 1). Though we touched on this concept in the previous chapter, it is crucial to understand what it means as we discuss the people component of the seeing clearly triad: principles, people and purpose. This type of love is called for within both leadership and consulting venues: "Love is a key ingredient of leadership" (Miller, 1995, p. 152), and "consulting at its best is an act of love: the wish to be genuinely helpful to another" (Block, 2000, p. xix). The love we speak of here then, is one where the leader considers "each employee/follower as a total person with needs, wants, and desires, [enabling the leader to go beyond] seeing people as hired hands, to seeing people as hired hearts" (Winston, 2002, p. 9). This concept is beautifully expressed in Blanchard and Barrett's (2011) *Lead with LUV* text: "Leadership is not about love—it *is* love. It's loving your mission, it's loving your customers, it's loving your people, and it's loving yourself enough to get out of the way so other people can be magnificent" (p. 22). As our second attribute of SC, seeing people, particularly all people in the organization, as hired hearts is what this love is about. What will this love inspire? Trust.

What enables a toddler to leap off a bed or off a pool's diving board into the waiting arms of their parent? It is the same enabler that dwells at the core between leaders and followers...trust. What is trust? One definition is, "confidence in or reliance on another team member" (Jacobs, 2006, p. 7).

The toddler trusts the parent to catch him or her. The parent trusts the toddler to have a vector that will enable catching the child, and trust that they have the ability to catch the child without harm. Following this leap of faith and trust, both parties rejoice! This example demonstrates a bi-directional nature of trust. It is similar to what we understand about leadership, that it is "a two-way interaction between leader and follower" (Winston, 2009, p. 2). Trust minimizes fear, and "fear is far more a liability than an asset where learning is involved" (Bell, 2002, p. 49). We will address the learning aspect in more detail later, but for now, we also realize that by minimizing fear, trust builds self-worth: "Taken in small increments of leaders trusting and empowering others this helps generate confidence in followers who may be frightened" (Winston & Patterson, 2006, p. 27). Not only does the leader become more confident in the follower, but the follower becomes more confident in himself and in the leader. We also realize that trust is easily broken…it is fragile. If the parent misses that child once or the leader is observed failing to walk the talk, then regaining trust will be an arduous process, if it is ever again achieved. Thus, the interplay of love, trust, and confidence is important if the leader is to successfully influence others. Trust acts as a safety net in the minds and hearts of employees. They may never need it, but are glad it exists, and because it exists, they are more likely to take risks that might benefit the organization. One might visualize a tightrope walker…a safety net may not be required, but it probably feels extremely good to have it beneath that walker. Not only does it feel good, but the walker can also focus more on what he or she is doing, and can take more risks. "Great organizations become great because the people inside the organization feel protected" (Sinek, 2011, p. 105).

One caution for the reader is necessary at this juncture. When we speak of love in this context, it does not indicate failing to uphold standards or cultural values. That is not the love of which we speak. Here is how Gordon Bethune, Continental Airlines CEO during its growth period, explained this aspect of the relationship with his employees:

We'd tell them about [our] Go Forward Plan. We'd patiently answer their questions. And if they wanted to say, "Well, you're just like all the others, you won't last long, I don't believe it," we'd listen. We couldn't really blame them. We'd make our pitch and hope to reach as many as we could. To be honest, employees who are too embittered and angry to listen—even with just cause—would probably be better off someplace else, and we'd probably be better off not trying to make them happy. Sometimes a company and an employee just don't mesh. (Bethune & Huler, 1998, p. 40)

Sometimes the love you must employ results in removing the employee. If the leader kept employees who either could not or would not abide by the principles set forth, what kind of example would that set for those remaining? Would that indicate that the leader was true to the principles espoused? Would that promote trust within the organization? Put succinctly, albeit perhaps a bit more harshly: "When people don't fit your company's culture, share them with the competition" (Blanchard & Barrett, 2011, p. 81).

With this understanding of what we mean by love, let us continue with our exploration of the verse by addressing the question: "Who is *our neighbor*?" Biblical references provide numerous examples of not only being a neighbor, but more importantly, being a *good neighbor*. For instance, we read the parable of the Good Samaritan:

Just then a lawyer stood up to test Jesus. "Teacher," he said, "what must I do to inherit eternal life?" He [Jesus] said to him [lawyer], "What is written in the law? What do you read there?" He answered, "You shall love the Lord your God with all your heart, and with all your soul, and with all your strength, and with all your mind; and your neighbor as yourself." And He [Jesus] said to him, "You have given the right answer; do this, and you will live." But wanting to justify himself, he asked Jesus, "And who is my neighbor?" Jesus replied, "A man was going down from Jerusalem to Jericho, and fell into the hands of robbers, who stripped him, beat him, and went away, leaving him half dead. Now by chance a priest was going down that road; and when he saw him, he passed by on the other side. So likewise a Levite, when he came to the place and saw him, passed by on the other side. But a Samaritan while traveling came near him; and when he saw him, he was moved with pity. He went to him and bandaged his wounds, having poured oil and wine on them. Then he put him on his own animal, brought him to an inn, and took care of him. The next day he took out two denarii, gave them to the innkeeper, and said, 'Take care of him; and when I come back, I will repay you whatever more you spend.' Which of these three, do you think, was a neighbor to the man who fell into the hands of the robbers?" He said, "The one who showed him mercy." Jesus said to him, "Go and do likewise." (Luke 10:25-37, Good News Bible)

From the above, the lawyer was able to discern that the neighbor was "the one who showed mercy to him [the traveler the Samaritan helped]" (Luke 10:37). Within that parable there were four characters: "1) the traveler [who was attacked]; 2) the priest who hastened past, probably not wishing to touch a dead man; 3) the Levite who perhaps went nearer to the traveler before moving on [without helping]; 4) the Samaritan, who would have been regarded by the Jews as the villain. [And we observed that] anyone from any nation who is in need is our neighbour" (Barclay, 2001, pp. 165-167). The priest and the Levite treated the man as a stranger, not wanting to get involved with his plight, not wanting to communicate with him to ascertain what his problem was, and to assist if able. However, the Samaritan communicated and acted as if the traveler was his neighbor, "having compassion" (Luke 10:33). The Samaritan even left money behind to ensure the traveler was taken care of and promised to reimburse the innkeeper (Luke 10:35). *Compassion* is an aspect of communicating with a person as a neighbor, as a hired heart, and not as a stranger. The opposite of compassion would be abuse, particularly as a leader expresses his or her power over the follower. It is a slippery slope to beware of, "beginning in our need for appreciation. From there the path winds upward to self-esteem...which...moves towards arrogance...arrogance disparages others and leads to abusive power" (Miller, 1995, p. 126). Miller coins a phrase that is worth remembering with regard to compassionless abuse of power: "'you-niverse' [sic] in which others exist solely to supply the advance of the power abuser" (Miller, 1995, p. 128). These leaders would view those in their employ as hired hands instead of hired hearts, as they view their workers as tools to prop up their own needs (e.g., financial, power, status, etc.). Miller also emphasizes: "Power is to be used only for the benefit of others, never for yourself" (Miller, 1995, p. 122). Leaders see clearly that compassion should be lavishly applied when interacting with neighbors.

This concept of neighbor is inclusive of *diversity*, which is part of God's plan, and therefore, it is a biblical principle relating to compassion and also being a good neighbor. The Samaritan in the above example was a foreigner to the man who was attacked. Elsewhere we are also told: "When God had finished creating the world, He looked at the 'vast array' (Gen 2:1) and announced that 'it was very good' (Gen 1:31). To celebrate creation is to celebrate diversity, including diversities of people" (Elmer, 1993, p. 13). These diverse people are our neighbors. As in the previous example with the lawyer, Jesus answers the question of which of God's Ten Commandments is the greatest, by condensing them to just two requirements: "Love the Lord your God with all your heart, with all your soul and with all your mind...love your neighbor as yourself" (Matt 22: 36-39). Loving one's neighbor is a requirement for all of mankind, to which leaders are included. Further, "love requires some understanding of its object. That means love is culturally defined. When we truly love others, we love them in their own context" (Elmer, 1993, p. 13). This implies a desire to get to know other cultures, which requires communication. Colleen Barrett, President Emeritus of Southwest Airlines expresses it this way:

> My biggest expectation with our people is that they be *egalitarian* in nature. When I use the word egalitarian, I mean that everybody has the right to be treated with respect, and everyone should be required to treat others with respect. And perhaps more importantly, everyone has an equal opportunity to contribute to the overall success and well-being of the company. (Blanchard & Barrett, 2011, p. 14)

Viewing people as hired hearts with an equal opportunity to contribute is an essential characteristic of this second leg of the SC triad. "Look after people and people will look after you was [Sam Walton's] belief, and everything Walton and Wal-Mart did proved it. It was people Walton valued above all else. People" (Sinek, 2011, p. 203). Though Walton was named in Forbes magazine as the richest man in America in 1985 (Sinek, 2011, p. 202), his focus was on people, not riches. His wealth was a *result* of his focus, but it was not his focus. This is a distinction that leaders must understand, and is worth repeating: wealth is the result of the organization's purpose; wealth is not the purpose of the organization.

Thus far, culture and communication have been introduced as we have discussed the meaning of "neighbor." Therefore, we must clearly see the interplay between communication and culture as they impact our ability to lead others...our neighbors. It is to this aspect that we now turn.

The Communication Imperative in a Shrinking World

Quite simply, how would a leader influence others without communicating? The leader's role is to steer the organization to achieve the purpose for which it exists, being a "decision shaper rather than a decision maker" (Galbraith, 2002, p. 180). This implies the ability to communicate with those being led. Another scholar puts the communication imperative for leaders this way: "There may be no single thing more important in our efforts to achieve meaningful work and fulfilling relationships than to learn and practice the art of communication" (DePree, 2004, p. 108). Research has shown, "lower and middle managers spend from 27 to 82 percent of their time engaged in oral communication and the figure was 65 to 75 percent for higher-level managers" (Yukl, 2010, p. 28). Five cross-cultural competencies are provided for leaders in the global marketplace:

- First, leaders need to understand business, political, and cultural environments worldwide;
- Second, they need to learn the perspective tastes, trends, and technologies of many other cultures;
- Third, they need to be able to work simultaneously with people from many cultures;
- Fourth, leaders must be able to adapt to living and communicating in other cultures;
- Fifth, they need to learn to relate to people from other cultures from a position of equality rather than cultural superiority. (Northouse, 2010, p. 335)

Communication is essential if one expects to influence a group of individuals to achieve a common goal. This text agrees with the notion offered by two scholars: "The process of communication is the same no matter whether the people with whom we are communicating come from our own culture (or group) or from a different culture (or group)" (Gudykunst & Kim, 2002, p. ix). Leaders seeking to have influence in their organizations and in the world should reflect upon that observation. Leaders should also consider the concept of communicating with those neighbors as a means of effectively managing and leading organizations—organizations increasingly consisting of various cultures and sub-cultures. This concept of communicating with neighbors is an imperative for leaders to see clearly—an essential approach for dealing with a world that is increasingly interconnected. Let us take a moment to reflect on this interconnectivity and what it bodes for communication efforts.

As we have stated previously, numerous scholars have pointed to what should be relatively obvious to the aware global citizen: that the world is becoming increasingly interconnected. Some cite two primary causal factors: "the electronic information revolution and global economic interdependence" (Rosen et al., 2000, p. 16). Others define those causes as: "technology, travel, trade, and television" (Marquardt & Berger, 2000, p. 3). Regardless of the approach, perhaps the increased degree of closeness humans have toward each other was first visualized globally in December 1968: "Ever since the first photograph of earth rising as seen from the moon, we've been awed by how small our planet really is…and the need for organizations to become global is now self-evident" (McCall & Hollenbeck, 2002, p. xvii). Not only our closeness, but also, perhaps, our universal insignificance was depicted when, from the vantage point of Earth's moon, an astronaut could completely block out the entire earth—where you and I, every world leader, and billions of our other neighbors reside—from view with his thumb.

This increased closeness, however, should not imply to the reader that things have become easier for any leader. The demands for effective communication are heightened, not reduced, within this new environment, driven by the above causal factors. For example, a technician halfway around the world, who is employed by the local company, could answer a service call for your television provider. This results in organizations that are quite literally without borders, and "this new borderless economy is changing faster than our ability to manage it. For companies to thrive, they must learn to excel in a multicultural world. They must also learn how to cross the new invisible borders of national culture" (Rosen et al., 2000, p. 20). We have already made the point that *trust mitigates fear, and fear is a liability where learning is involved.* Companies will require savvy leaders that can see clearly how to steer—through effective communication—their organizations across those invisible borders. The leaders will need to view multiculturalism that will undoubtedly arise as an opportunity for communicating with neighbors, not strangers, some, perhaps many of whom the leader may have no personal acquaintance.

It should be clear that the leader must be able to communicate to the follower to garner their understanding and agreement in order for the organization's purpose to be fulfilled. As a matter of introduction to a later discussion, the global leader must develop an understanding of the context or environment both internal to, and external from the organization to facilitate establishing the objectives of the organization. This takes desire, effort and time: "Global leaders are content with nothing less than learning the feel of the very texture of any place they work in, any country they visit" (Black, Morrison, & Gregersen, 1999, p. 50); "the needed characteristics cannot be developed overnight" (Black et al., 1999, p. 36). If these characteristics, and in particular, communication capabilities, can be developed, this supports the implication that global leadership qualities can be learned, which is why the emphasis is on including this aspect of SC. Unlike the manner in which some leaders are viewed, these needed characteristics are not necessarily a birthright, but can be learned. Being able to effectively communicate is an imperative for influencing others, including those of different cultures. Though we are interconnected and indeed close, there are cultural differences we must see clearly as we interact and communicate both as a leader and also as a follower.

As we develop this understanding of culture, communication and the leader's role, there are ten assumptions leaders may make that should be avoided when doing business with other cultures:

1. Thinking the world plays by your rules—the Global Competitiveness Report 2013-2014 assesses the competitiveness landscape of 148 economies. The latest report ranks the United States as fifth behind Switzerland, Singapore, Finland, and Germany (Schwab, 2014, p. 15);
2. Doing what you always did in the past;
3. Taking English for granted, and as we will see shortly, language reflects culture, and culture reflects language;
4. Not respecting the cultural pathways for making things happen, for example, the French boycotted the inauguration of Euro Disney in large part because the kiosks failed to serve wine and local food that French people love;
5. Not standing in your host's shoes and failing to consult with other cultures when formulating plans;
6. Forgetting to invest in relationships;
7. Leaping from vision to action, even in Central and Northern Europe, the "how" must be crystal clear to people before they take action;
8. Taking the village by storm;
9. Selecting the wrong people, those who may have technical merit, while not considering their cross-cultural expertise; and
10. Forgetting that your advice may be noise in their ears, that perhaps asking questions and listening is what is most desired. (Zweifel, 2003, pp. 21-35)

There are some key elements an individual might engage in to increase their leadership capabilities in the global environment, and, thus, avoid the preceding faulty assumptions:

1. Examination: learning from experiences through introspection and self-awareness;
2. Education: proactively learning the language and customs of the various cultures;
3. Experience: actively seeking to participate in diverse meetings that are relevant, meaningful, and applied; and
4. Exposure: having mentors that have "been there, done that" and living or frequently visiting other cultures so as to be immersed in them. (Cohen, 2010, p. 8)

In order to accomplish the above, leaders need certain attributes, which are primarily parts of their personality:

1. Inquisitiveness: more of an attitude than a skill. Think of healthy babies, and how they develop and learn. This can be thought of as having a healthy desire to learn new things and not approach differences as "drudgery;"
2. Perspective: which is how one views the world. This requires the ability to embrace uncertainty and balance tensions as they arise, using innovation to balance competing demands;
3. Character: which consists of one's emotional connection and unwavering integrity. Which is again why we explored principles first as an essential step for leaders. They are keys to inspiring goodwill and trust, which are freely given, not commanded or controlled;
4. Savvy: to be discussed in a following chapter, but pertains to business and organizational skills to know what needs to be done and what resources are required to make it happen. (Black et al., 1999, p. xi)

Communication, therefore, is *how* we influence others, and this communication springs from our hearts to theirs, "for the mouth speaks what the heart is full of" (Matthew 12:34, NIV), and "the things that come out of a person's mouth come from the heart" (Matthew 15:18, NIV). This is why we spent time within the first chapter developing those principles that will serve our hearts as we seek to influence others. But there is more we should concern ourselves with as we continue to explore communication. There is more to develop for the leader to be able to see this aspect clearly.

Culture is Communication and Communication is Culture

Culture can be examined in many ways, such as "the set of values, norms guiding beliefs, and understandings that is shared by members of an organization and taught to new members as the correct way to think, feel, and behave" (Daft, 2010, p. 374). As with the iceberg discussed in the principles chapter, there are both visible and invisible behaviors relating to culture. The underlying values, norms, assumptions, beliefs, understandings, attitudes and feelings within the underwater portion are likely to be enormous in comparison to what may be apparent on the surface.

Culture is the context in which we live, the windows through which we experience the world: our attitudes (judgments about people, places, and cultures), our values (desires, wants, and needs), and our identities (who we are and who they are). All are part of the many layers of culture, whether national, linguistic, corporate, ethnic, racial or individual. (Rosen et al., 2000, p. 33)

It is important for the leader to clearly see and understand not only her own cultural biases and norms, but also those of the follower, and by extension, the external environment. She takes the time to consider her own personal attitudes, values, and identities, and also those of the internal customer (employees) and the external customer as well. This is an ever-increasing need due to the global interconnectivity previously discussed. Not seeing cultural differences clearly can have derailing impacts on the ability of the organization to fulfill its purpose. This derailment may be due to what is communicated to the audience (often unwittingly), as these examples indicate:

- McDonald's took thirteen months to realize that Hindus in India don't eat beef. When it started making hamburgers out of lamb, sales flourished;
- In Africa, companies show pictures of what's inside bottles so illiterate customers know what they're getting. When a baby food company showed a picture of a child on its label, little wonder the product didn't sell very well;
- An American television ad for deodorant depicted an octopus putting antiperspirant under each arm. When the ad flopped in Japan, the producers realized that octopuses don't have arms, they have legs. (Rosen et al., 2000, p. 176)

We sometimes find that culture has been described as "analogous to music. If a person hasn't heard music, it is impossible to describe" (Hall, 1959, p. xviii). Culture, therefore, has many attributes. It is not necessarily confined to national borders, and it affects how people think and act, to include how people communicate. It is as much a reflection of a group as personality traits reflect an individual. As one's personality communicates something about an individual, so too does culture communicate something pertaining to that group. "Hofstede states that culture is to a human collectivity what personality is to an individual" (Sharpe, 1981, p. 24). For others, "culture is a mold in which we are all cast, and it controls our daily lives in many unexpected ways" (Hall, 1959, p. 30); "the very patterns of thinking vary from culture to culture because they are culturally constructed" (Zweifel, 2003, p. 15); and, perhaps, most critically for the global leader, "behavior that is acceptable in one culture can become a derailer [sic] in another" (McCall & Hollenbeck, 2002, p. 12).

Since we have stated that our world is shrinking, should not cultural differences be reduced? "Hardly. As our national borders dissolve, we assert our cultural ones more fiercely" (Rosen et al., 2000, p. 32). Scholars also emphasize cultural differences are not only emotional and intellectual (Hall, 1959, p. 59; McCall & Hollenbeck, 2002, p. 31), they are very deeply rooted. "Culture is not one thing but a complex series of activities interrelated in many ways, activities with origins deeply buried in a past when there were no cultures and no men" (Hall, 1959, p. 58).

Several studies have attempted to determine how cultures affect or influence management and organizations. One such study was Project GLOBE, which reviewed 62 cultures. That study examined cultures from several vantage points, or dimensions, as indicated in Table 2.

Table 2. GLOBE Study—Cultural Dimensions

Dimension	Definition
* Power distance	The degree to which members of a society expect power to be distributed equally
* Uncertainty avoidance	The extent to which a society relies on social norms, rules and procedures to alleviate unpredictability of future events
Humane orientation	The degree to which a society encourages and rewards individuals for being fair, altruistic, generous, caring and kind to others
Institutional collectivism	The degree to which societal institutional practices encourage and reward collective distribution of resources and collective action
In-group collectivism	The degree to which individuals express pride, loyalty and cohesiveness in their families
Assertiveness	The degree to which individuals are assertive, dominant and demanding in their relationships with others
Gender egalitarianism	The degree to which a society minimizes gender inequality
Future orientation	The extent to which a society encourages future-orientated behaviors such as delaying gratification, planning and investing in the future
Performance orientation	The degree to which a society encourages and rewards group members for performance improvement and excellence

[Adapted from: House, R. J., Hanges, P. J., Javidan, M., Dorfman, P. W., & Gupta, V. (2004).
Culture, leadership and organizations: The GLOBE study of 62 societies.]

To understand the implications of the above, consider the uncertainty avoidance cultural dimension. It may also be stated as "The extent to which members of a society [culture] strive to avoid uncertainty by relying on established norms, rituals and bureaucratic processes" (House, Hanges, Javidan, Dorfman, & Gupta, 2004, p. 11). The nature of uncertainty avoidance rests in the group's willingness to take risks in the face of ambiguity. To highlight its impact, for example, if the leader is communicating a need for creativity, there probably will be ambiguity, a trait of creative activities. A culture that is risk averse would not necessarily be inclined toward creative efforts, just due to the uncertainty of those efforts. The GLOBE study found "Southern Asia, Middle East, Sub-Saharan Africa, Eastern Europe, and Latin America scoring relatively high on uncertainty avoidance, whereas Northern European and Anglo societies scored relatively low" (House et al., 2004, p. 635). Does this mean that creativity is out of the question for those cultures scoring high in this area? Not in the slightest, however, the method of communicating to these cultures should reflect an understanding this cultural dimension implies.

Gerard Hendrik (Geert) Hofstede is a Dutch social psychologist and is one of the most cited scholars when addressing national cultural issues. His original quantitative model is similar to what we presented above in the GLOBE Study, but is based on four dimensions of national culture. Significantly, "the country scores provided by Hofstede have been extensively adopted in studies on national culture to show the impacts on 'management practices' in terms of strategy style of leadership, organizational practices, HRM [Human Resource Management], and new product development" (Cagliano, Caniato, Golini, Longoni, & Micelotta, 2011, p. 300). Two of Hofstede's dimensions are similar to what we defined above within the GLOBE study, and are asterisked in Table 2 (Power Distance and Uncertainty Avoidance). Due to its widespread use in a number of fields, we will use Hofstede's four dimensions, depicted in Table 3, to explore six cultures as they might relate to the United States, and to highlight why cultural differences should not be taken for granted, particularly when communicating.

Table 3. Hofstede's Dimensions of National Culture

Dimension	Description
Power distance	Reflects inequality in power depending on prestige, influence, wealth, and status. High-power distance societies tend to use more coercive and referent power, whereas low-power distance societies use more legitimate power.
Individualism	Describes the relationship between the individual and the collective. A given society's norm for individualism versus collectivism will strongly affect the nature of the relationship between people and the organization to which they belong.
Masculinity	Related to the evidence that dissimilar societies cope differently with gender roles. In countries with a lower masculinity index (higher levels of femininity), life satisfaction of workers tends to take precedence over job success.
Uncertainty avoidance	Measures the extent to which countries deem the pursuit of certainty important. Cultures with high uncertainty avoidance reveal a preference for long-term predictability of rules, work arrangements, and relationships, as well as an avoidance of risk-taking

[Adapted from: Cagliano, R., et al. (2011). The impact of country culture on the adoption of new forms of work organization. *International Journal of Operations & Production Management*.]

Figure 1 displays Hofstede's scoring of seven cultures, including the United States. We will baseline the discussion around the scores for the United States and then highlight some differences for the selected nations. The nations were selected to provide the reader with cultural examples from neighbors, to include neighbors whose economic, social, or political views the United States may oppose. Even for cultures one might assume are "just like ours," we can see that there are differences of which we should be aware if our communication with them is to be effective. We must continue to see clearly that leaders seek to *influence*, which mandates *effective communication*.

Figure 1. Utilizing Hofstede's Cultural Dimensions to Compare Seven Nations

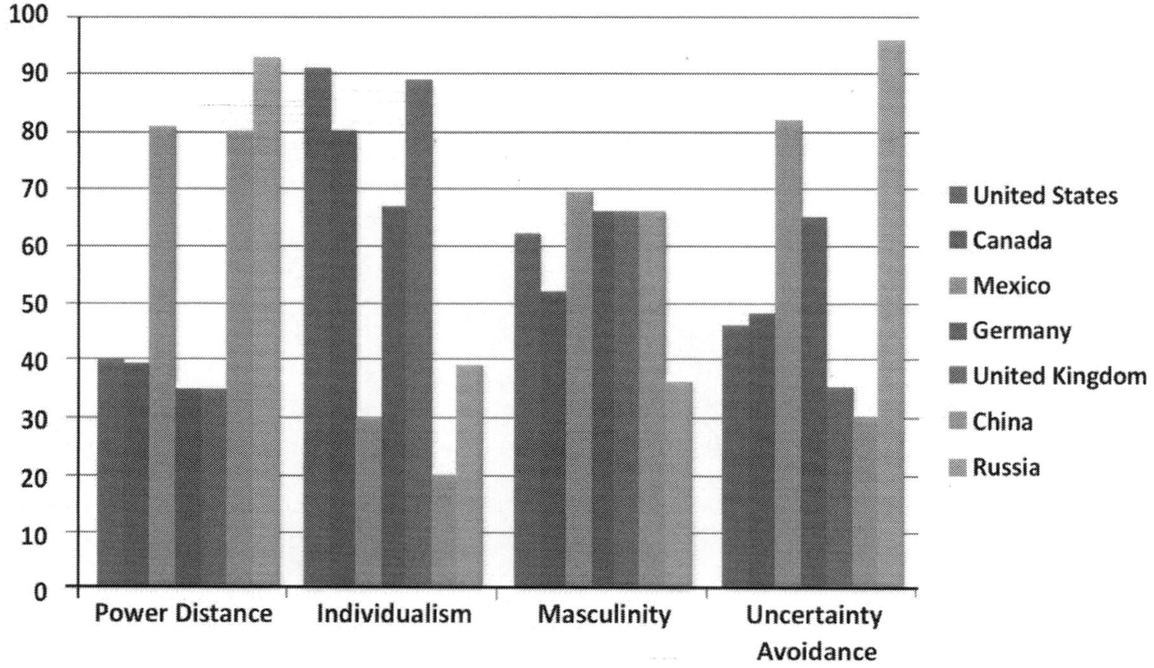

[Extracted from: Geert Hofstede – http://geert-hofstede.com on May 11, 2014]

Power Distance: The first few words in the second paragraph of the American Declaration of Independence speak volumes of why the United States has a fairly low score for this dimension: "We hold these truths to be self-evident, that all men are created equal, that they are endowed by their Creator with certain unalienable Rights." Americans believe it is *self-evident that a Creator creates all men equal,* and that there are *certain rights that are unalterable by man.* As such, as a nation, we strive to equalize power distribution and even more, demand justification wherever there are inequalities of power. It matters not whether one is a follower or a leader—inequality is fervently fought against.

Individualism: This can simply be examined as to whether people's self-image is based or defined in terms of "I" or "we." Here, America scores quite high. Individual achievement is sought. We may laud a particular sports team, but we tend to place on a higher pedestal specific individuals on those teams. For example, the quarterback on a football team could do nothing without full support of the team members, but we seem to rest winning or losing on the person in that quarterback position.

Masculinity: This dimension concerns whether the society will be driven by competition, achievement, or success. America has a relatively high score in this area. Clearly, the American dream is one of improving one's lot in life from a financial perspective. This drives Americans to typically be seen as "living to work," to be able to beat the competition, to have achievements, and to become regarded as successful. We can see this aspect play upon the viewer's psyche with television commercials where that viewer is bombarded with various means of demonstrating their success, such as a better car, nicer house, snappier clothes, etc. In a general sense, it isn't enough to be successful in America, one has to demonstrate success by their possessions.

Uncertainty Avoidance – Since the future is unknown, Americans are relatively accepting of new ideas, innovation and just trying something new. The fairly low score supports the entrepreneurial spirit and willingness to take risks found in America as compared to other national cultures. Quite vividly, our history of expanding this nation from the eastern shore to the Pacific coast is an example of this "spirit of exploration in the face of uncertainty" that exists within America.

Though it may seem obvious, we must take the time to understand our own culture as a baseline because, "The analysis of one's own culture simply makes explicit the many things we take for granted in our everyday lives. Talking about them, however, changes our relation with them" (Hall, 1959, p. 140). This takes us all the way back to the concept of "removing logs from our own eyes," as we seek to clearly see ourselves before analyzing others. Though we will not dwell here, this is a daunting challenge as "culture hides most effectively from its own participants" (Hall, 1959, p. 30). With those points emphasized, Table 4 contains explanations of the remaining six referenced nations (cultures), to include communication implications. As one reviews any of this data, it is important to remember that these are generalizations pertaining to the various cultures as a whole and may not be experienced in a particular one-on-one situation. They are offered and suggested to provide context and an initial understanding of how to communicate, as those cultural differences have an impact on how one should approach communication. The take away or the "So what?" of this is to see clearly that other cultures, even those who we presume are similar to our own, may not see things as we do due to their cultural differences; this will affect how we communicate with them, and them with us. As a side note, these very same differences may lie *within* various cultures, organizations, or groups.

Table 4. Hofstede's Cultural Dimensions and Communication Implications

Country	Power Distance	Individualism	Masculinity	Uncertainty Avoidance	Communication Implication
Canada	*Low* Value placed on egalitarianism	*High* - Self-reliant and display initiative	*Moderately masculine society;* have a work-life balance and are likely to take time to enjoy life in general	*Uncertainty accepting;* tolerant of ideas or opinions from anyone and allow freedom of expression	Value a straightforward exchange of information
Mexico	*High* - Hierarchical society; subordinates expect to be told what to do; the ideal boss is a benevolent autocrat	*Low* - Collectivistic society; long-term commitment to the member group; offense leads to shame and loss of face	*Masculine society;* live in order to work; managers are expected to be decisive and assertive	*Very high preference for avoiding uncertainty;* intolerant of unorthodox behavior and ideas; emotional need for rules	When communicating, precision and punctuality are the norm, innovation efforts may be resisted
Germany	*Low* - Highly decentralized; leadership is challenged to show expertise	*High –* Individualistic; strong belief in the idea of self-actualization	*Masculine society;* draw a lot of self-esteem from their tasks; status displayed, especially by cars, watches and technical devices	*Preference for uncertainty avoidance;* preference for deductive rather than inductive approaches	Direct and participative communication and meeting style is common, control is disliked; "be honest, even if it hurts"
United Kingdom	*Low -* Inequalities among people should be minimized	*High* - Highly individualistic and private	*Masculine society -* highly success oriented and driven	*Comfortable in ambiguous situations;* the term "muddling through" is a very British way of expressing this	Combination of a highly individualistic, private and curious nation results in high level of creativity and strong innovation need
China	*High -* Inequalities among people acceptable; people should not have aspirations beyond rank	*Low* - Highly collectivist culture; personal relationships prevail over task and company	*Masculine society -* success oriented and driven; will sacrifice family and leisure priorities to work	*Comfortable with ambiguity*	Chinese language is full of ambiguous meanings that can be difficult for Western people to follow
Russia	*Very high -* Power is very distant in society	*Low -* Relationships crucial in obtaining information, getting introduced or successful negotiations	*Feminine society -* understate their personal achievements, contributions or capacities	*Threatened by ambiguous situations;* presentations either not prepared, e.g. when negotiations started and the focus is on relationship building, or extremely detailed and well prepared	Communication must reflect and represent the status roles in all areas of business interactions; personal, authentic and trustful communication is essential before focusing on tasks

[Extracted from: Geert Hofstede – http://geert-hofstede.com on May 11, 2014]

Given the above discussion, it would be reasonable at this juncture to provide examples of how the interplay of one's culture may affect their worldview, and hence, communication. Let us look at a simple example of how cultures may view time as it pertains to communication efforts. For the United States, "time is handled much like material; we earn it, spend it, save it, waste it" (Hall, 1959, p. 7). Another culture, perhaps one Americans hope to do business with, may view relationships (e.g., Mexico, China, and Russia, as indicated in Table 4) to be more important than the American culture views time, which might impact how they perceive our communication with them. For example, Americans may become antsy, perhaps even irate, if they are kept waiting longer than five minutes for an appointment. This level of irritation could be communicated non-verbally (or verbally) to the other party as a negative attribute, thereby placing a rift in the relationship or business. Note in this example, the rift may arise without a word being said…but that does not mean that communication has not occurred! One's body language or facial expression may be all the communication that is necessary to express frustration with that five-minute delay. While examining this view of time with more scrutiny, scholars postulate:

> People with a monochronic orientation [towards time] are task-oriented, emphasize promptness and a concern for others' privacy, stick to their plans, seldom borrow or lend private property, and are accustomed to short-term relationships with other people. Conversely, people with a polychronic orientation tend to change plans, borrow and lend things frequently, emphasize relationships rather than tasks and privacy, and build long-term relationships with family members, friends, and business partners. (Bluedorn, Kaufman, & Lane, 1992, p. 19)

Scholars realize the importance of being able to distinguish between cultures as a vital element of leadership, and by the preceding examples, it is evident that leaders also must see this clearly:

> Given the increasingly international nature of business and management, the strategic competitive advantages will be held by the individuals, companies, and nations who learn how to successfully manage cultural diversity. And temporal differences such as monochronic/polychronic orientations are among the most basic cultural differences to manage. (Bluedorn et al., 1992, p. 25)

Thus, a relatively simple thing as the manner in which a culture views time could create communication challenges for the leader when interacting with other cultures, specifically ones who view time differently. Therefore, in order to be effective across a broad range of cultures, leaders must consider and develop an understanding of those differences to enable effective communication. Culture is communication. However, even Hofstede's "dimension approach does not replace in-depth studies of country cultures; on the contrary, it invites them...cultural dimensions were never intended to provide a complete basis for analyzing a culture"(Hofstede & Peterson, 2000, p. 404). Stated alternatively, "any study attempting to characterize a given culture is complicated and risky. No one is simply a product of his or her culture" (Rosen et al., 2000, p. 10). The generalizations and dimensions are not meant to imply that leaders should not attempt to see clearly the nature of the people they are specifically dealing with on an individual basis. However, they do provide broad guidelines as one communicates with people from other cultures, and we communicate through language. As we will see next, language as the means of communicating, can either be verbal or silent (non-verbal).

"Language is the expression of culture, enabling us to communicate through the ages with people who share our history and identity" (Rosen et al., 2000, p. 57). As we read the biblical story of Creation, we get a glimpse of just how important communication and language are. God *spoke* creation into being commencing with: "Let there be light" (Gen 1:3, NIV). Within the New Testament, referring to Jesus, the Apostle John tells the reader: "In the beginning was the *Word*, and the *Word* was with God and the *Word was God* [emphasis added]" (John 1:1, NIV). These are two powerful biblical excerpts displaying the power of speech and of words—communication and language as the means of communicating.

Regarding cultural effects on communication, "George Bernard Shaw said, the single biggest problem in communication is the illusion that it has taken place" (Hoover, 2010, p. 20). Previously, we saw the example of the American baby food company in Africa, and the miscommunication that arose because the baby food company placed a picture of a baby on the label, whereas the culture "expected" a picture of the contents on the label. The baby food company was under the illusion that what they intended to communicate was communicated. But they were quite incorrect!

Just like culture, there are many aspects to observing communication. However one choses to view it, it is essential to building an environment where the organization's purpose may be achieved: "To create a culture of trust, leaders need to be authentic, credible, and in integrity—communicating honestly" (Kelly, 2007, p. 13). Communicating what the leader intends when cultures are different is a challenge, but the leader who can accomplish this will enhance opportunities for the organization's success and minimize cultural conflict. Additionally, as organizations grow, "an increasingly large part that communication plays in expanding culture is to pass along values to new members and reaffirm those values to old hands" (DePree, 2004, p. 108). As we surveyed Table 4, we saw examples of several of the following areas of disagreement, which negatively affect productive communication:

Common areas of communication disagreement among cultures include the following: willingness to openly disagree; the importance of maintaining "face," or dignity; the way agreement is defined; the amount of time devoted to establishing personal relationships; willingness to speak assertively; mode of communication; personal space and nonverbal communication. (Hitt, Miller, & Colella, 2009, p. 58)

The preceding comment should provide a clear understanding of the verbal concerns of communication as they apply to culture. Another scholar explores what is coined the "silent language" of communication. Here we see how these five silent language factors relate to a discussion of communication as a culture. These factors also support why being able to see people as neighbors is important to the leader in a multi-cultural world.

• *The language of time* has already been addressed in the discussion of monochronic and polychronic views of time. Delays in answering a communication in the United States may be non-verbally understood to display a lack of interest. However, "a similar delay in a foreign country may mean something altogether different" (Hall, 1960, p. 88). "To the old-time Navajo time is like space—only the here and now is quite real. What would you think of a people who had no word for time? The future has little reality to it" (Hall, 1959, pp. 13-14). On the other hand, for Americans, "the future to us is in the foreseeable future, not the future of the South Asian that may involve centuries" (Hall, 1959, p. 8). Another example to highlight this difference might include American views on haggling or bargaining for an item, which might be considered as a waste of time. "To the Arab, bargaining is not only a means of passing a day but actually is a technique of interpersonal relations" (Hall, 1959, p. 107).

• *The language of space* is different depending on the culture. "Americans have no difficulty in appraising the relative importance of someone else, simply by noting the size of the office in relation to other offices around that person" (Hall, 1960, p. 90). In the United States, a mark of success could be to have the corner office on the top floor of the corporation. However, in countries like France, the supervisor, rather than having that "corner office on the top floor," as might be expected in the U.S., may be found in the middle of subordinates in order to facilitate control of them. They view the usage of space quite differently. "In French offices the key figure is the man in the middle, who has his fingers on everything so that all runs smoothly" (Hall, 1959, p. 176). The next example may be initially viewed as comical, but space also speaks regarding the distance people are from each other when conversing. "In Latin America, the interaction distance is much less than in the United States. The result is that when they move close, we [Americans] withdraw and back away. As a consequence, they think we are distant or cold, withdrawn and unfriendly" (Hall, 1959, p. 185). By backing up into what we as Americans think is our personal space, we may silently send a poor message to others who view that space differently.

• *The language of things* is a trait typical to Americans. One potential reason for this may be as a result of our low power distance. "Lacking a fixed class system and having an extremely mobile population, Americans have become highly sensitive to how others make use of material possessions" (Hall, 1960, p. 91). This results in things being used as a measure of status. "We use everything from clothes to houses as a highly evolved and complex means of ascertaining each other's status…[in contrast] the Japanese take pride in often inexpensive but tasteful arrangements that are used to produce the proper emotional setting" (Hall, 1960, p. 91). We have already seen within Table 4 that the German culture also uses things to express success and self-esteem (e.g., cars, watches). We also noted that for the Chinese, their interest is in forming a relationship, not impressing others with physical items, to be used as status symbols.

• *The language of friendship* is fleeting in America. "We take people up quickly and drop them just as quickly. Occasionally a friendship formed during schooldays will persist, but this is rare…as a general rule friendships in foreign countries are not formed as quickly but go much deeper, last longer, and involve real obligations" (Hall, 1960, p. 91). This connects back to the language of time, as developing relationships would take time, something Americans may not be predisposed to commit to. Failing to take that time and make that effort to form personal relationships would affect how another culture views the American leader. They might be more interested in forming a relationship prior to conducting business, where the American may be inclined to just get the job done.

• *The language of agreements* concerns those rules for negotiating agreements in various cultures. The American view "lays heavy emphasis on rules that are spelled out technically as law or regulation, such as a contract…in the Arab world, once a man's word is given in a particular kind of way, it is just as binding, if not more so, than most of our written contracts" (Hall, 1960, p. 92). This issue could result in serious problems if one party assumes an agreement was made, and the other does not. The American penchant for contracts and litigation may be offensive to other cultures where a handshake is binding.

While keeping the above communication points in mind, the leader should also remember they indeed remain the leader, responsible for the success or failure of their organization. Being able to communicate with followers does not alleviate the leader from the leadership role. Having rapport with subordinates does not obviate the leader from their responsibilities. Since the leader seeks to influence, the burden of communicating effectively falls upon that station:

Leaders who are interested in people, who are excellent listeners, and who are familiar with local conditions do not have to become like the people they are with. While you need to change parts of yourself that interfere with communication and are obstacles to empathy, you cannot lose sight of your position as a leader. (Black et al., 1999, p.127)

Let us look at an ancient example of how a simple communication event can be totally misconstrued based upon a cultural view. It illustrates that what one may think has been communicated is not always what was communicated. While examining this brief example, remember, "like a telephone system, any communication system has three aspects: its over-all structure, comparable to the telephone network; its components, comparable to switchboards, wires, and telephones; and the message itself, which is carried by the network" (Hall, 1959, p. 100). Communication and culture are intertwined such that communication is culture, and culture is communication. If one treats that different culture as a neighbor, opportunities for mutual understanding would be enhanced, as would the success of the organization's mission.

A biblical example of the interplay of communication and culture, and how to communicate as if a neighbor is found in John 4:1-42. These verses provide an account of Jesus' interaction with a Samaritan woman at a well and the resulting impact. Jesus was traveling from Judea to Galilee, via a direct route through Samaria. "Though Samaria was the most direct route from Judea to Galilee, strict Jews, wishing to avoid defilement, bypassed Samaria by taking a longer, more direct route"

(*HCSB Study Bible, Holman Christian Standard Bible: God's word for life*, 2010, p. 1809). While there, Jesus met and conversed with a Samaritan woman, who somehow recognized (we are not told how she did so within the biblical text) Jesus as a Jew. She also understood how Jews viewed Samaritans, where even speaking to her (a Samaritan) was outside of the norm. As the dialogue begins, the woman initially speaks to Jesus as a stranger. She treats Him with a degree of wariness and perhaps suspicion, but Jesus communicated with her as a friend and neighbor, breaking down all barriers she may have raised by His actions and words. He told her many things she did not expect Him to know. He is aware that she had five husbands and was now living with a man who is not her husband. Jesus is aware of the vast cultural differences between the Jews and the Samaritans, and quite literally meets this woman where she is. Through the ensuing dialogue, the woman becomes amazed at Jesus and actually goes back into town (called "Sychar") to gather people to come see Him. Even Jesus' disciples, returning to Jesus after looking for food, were amazed that Jesus would have conversed with that Samaritan woman. Jesus stayed in that town with those people for two days, and more and more people believed in Him because of what and how He communicated with them: "Many more believed because of what He said" (John 4:41, HCSB). Thus, despite cultural differences, Jesus spoke to the Samaritan woman and ultimately the Samaritan townspeople as neighbors, bringing many to His mission. Jesus, God's only Son, communicated with people as neighbors, not as strangers. As a result of this and many acts, thousands of years later, His three-year earthly mission has impacted billions of people.

Today, there is no question that improved technology, communication methods, travel abilities, and other marvels, make the world and its occupants seem closer, perhaps more in touch or interconnected than ever before. However, as we have stated previously, these conditions do not mean there will no longer be cultural differences. Evidence indicates quite the contrary.

The effective leader will not view people from other cultures as strangers but as neighbors, with a desire to get to know them that comes from the heart. "Heart" brings forth the notion of empathy and sensitivity towards others, and is where the idea of loving one's neighbor dwells. This leader must remember, "in the collection of information on a culture, the inquirer must proceed with empathy in order to perceive [the culture's] cardinal values (Kroeber & Kluckhohn, 1952, p. 173). In doing so, they will see that by being "sensitive to people, they will, by definition, also be sensitive to the cultures from which they come" (McCall & Hollenbeck, 2002, p. 89). By their actions as well as their words (non-verbal as well as verbal), it will be observed that, as effective leaders, they actually like understanding their neighbor (follower) while building the organization's success. This desire to understand others serves to enhance communication, which has the great potential to increase the leader's influence. "Various studies have highlighted the importance of communication for the success of the organization, and have shown that quality of communication in organizations are associated with employee job satisfaction and motivation" (Sarangi & Srivastava, 2012, p. 22).

These same leaders understand, "there is a proper analogy between cultures and personalities. Each human being is unique in his concrete totality, yet he resembles all other human beings in certain respects" (Kroeber & Kluckhohn, 1952, p. 179). One might draw the same comparison toward cultures. They are each unique, yet they may resemble others. Ultimately, leaders could use the concept of communicating with neighbors as a means to get to understand their neighbor's culture better. By understanding the culture better, by seeing them more clearly (without presumptions or assumptions, but with a desire filled with empathy), there is a greater opportunity for improved communication. With better communication, the leader creates increased opportunities to influence. This all results from treating followers as the leader would like to be treated, as individuals worthy of the respect and care originally designed for all men, in the beginning, when it was very good.

Succession—The Leader's Legacy

As a leader gazes across the expanse of her organization, she must realize and understand that her days as the leader are numbered. Consider the following concerning where we are today as a human race:

If the last 50,000 years of man's existence were divided into lifetimes of approximately sixty-two years each there have been about 800 such lifetimes...of these 800, fully 650 were spent in caves...only during the last six did masses of men see a printed word...only during the last four has it been possible to measure time with any precision...only in the last two has anyone anywhere used an electric motor...the overwhelming majority of all the material goods we use in daily life today have been developed within the present, the 800th lifetime. (Toffler, 1971, p. 14)

The above comment is a sobering one that we typically take for granted. Many have the assumption that things have always been as they are, and even worse, that they will always continue as they are at present. Retirement, transitioning to another job, the organization's realignment with another organization, or perhaps a calamity, will impact a leader's tenure. For example, "when the World Trade Center was destroyed, 172 corporate vice presidents lost their lives" (Rothwell, 2005, p. xvii). It is for the above reasons and many more, why "choosing leaders is the most vital and important matter corporations and institutions face" (DePree, 2004, p. 134). As with everything we have discussed concerning the people attribute of SC, leaders are responsible for future leadership. They need to identify, develop and nurture future leaders. Leaders must clearly see the necessity, the means and the methods for developing leaders within their organization, and this implies some sort of succession plan. There are some, albeit currently successful leaders, who fail to comprehend this need.

Sheldon Adelson is the Chairman and CEO of Las Vegas Sands. As of September 2013, this 80-year-old businessman was listed in *Forbes* as the 11th richest American with a net worth of $28.5B ("Sheldon Adelson," 2013). He is quoted as saying, "Why do I need succession planning? I'm very alert, I'm very vibrant. I have no intention to retire" (Adelson, n.d.). One might offer that the 172 corporate vice presidents mentioned above had no intention of retiring on September 11, 2001 either. Consider the situation arising from Commerce Secretary Ron Brown's 1996 airplane crash in Croatia, which killed 34 people, including 12 senior executives from a variety of organizations (Rothwell, 2005, p. 67). Of course, circumstances need not be that dire within an organization for succession planning to be a good approach, and it is part and parcel of looking at followers as more than hired hands, but as hired hearts upon whom the leader's legacy is sustained.

Leaders are responsible for tangible assets such as, "financial health, services, products and the tools and equipment people in the organization need" (DePree, 2004, p. 13). Additionally, leaders are responsible for human capital in the form of future leadership. "They need to identify, develop, and nurture future leaders" (DePree, 2004, p. 14). Human capital is "the productive capacity imbedded in an individual that results from natural capability, education, and experience" (Nelson, 2000, p. 138). Human capital is an intangible resource leaders must consider. As one successful business executive stated, "Burn down my buildings and give me my people, and we'll rebuild the company in a year. But leave my buildings and take away the people…and I'll have a real problem" (Nelson, 2000, p. 139). The leader's legacy survives with the organization's properly trained and motivated people, and a succession plan is part of that training and motivation.

Focusing on the intangible asset, the organization's people, promises to provide the competitive advantage an organization requires. Competitive advantage is "what sets the organization apart from others and provides it with a distinctive edge for meeting customer or client needs in the marketplace" (Daft, 2010, p. 61). Paradoxically, many leaders who purport, "people are our most important asset" often do little to acquire or prepare those same people to enable maximum competitive advantage. All too often they view people as hired hands, not hired hearts, as commodities, not comrades fulfilling a common purpose. "Companies don't hire, promote, and develop the best candidates for their leadership needs" (Bossidy & Charan, 2009, p. 109). This is the issue succession planning seeks to address; why it is a critical need within all organizations; and why leaders must clearly see its importance while giving it their full attention.

As we saw during discussions concerning the definition of leadership, *succession planning is a process*, not necessarily a singular event. "Succession planning is a process of developing talent to meet the needs of the organization now and in the future. Every time a manager makes a work assignment, he or she is preparing someone for the future because he or she is building that worker's ability" (Rothwell, 2005, p. 389). As the definition indicates, it does not solely apply to the CEO or upper leadership positions. Consider the following.

Hearst Corporation is a media and information company with revenues of $3.9B as of December 2013 ("America's largest private companies," n.d.). It is more than 125 years old and it consists of 20,000 employees in 171 countries. During the summer of 2013, there was a CEO handoff from Frank Bennack Jr. to Steven Swartz. Bennack recalls his predecessor (John Miller) telling him, "You will do things with the company that I won't do. That's what needs to happen to the company, so I'm going to retire" (Kowitt, 2013, p. 143). When Bennack took the reins, "one of his first orders of business was filling a gap in a missing generation of leadership. It was a necessary move if he was going to get succession right" (Kowitt, 2013, p. 144). Unlike the earlier referenced remarks from Las Vegas Sands' CEO Adelson, Bennack proceeded to consider and mentor his successor: "Every transaction, every personnel move, every important decision, we talked about together" (Kowitt, 2013, p. 144). Swartz had started as a reporter for the Wall Street Journal, eventually becoming founding editor and CEO of SmartMoney Magazine and website before transitioning to Hearst. Bennack attracted, developed, and retained the talent he needed to run the organization (Swartz), looking ahead to his ultimate retirement. The steps Bennack took are the essence of succession planning, and are useful within all levels of the organization:

1.   Attract talent by understanding not only what the organization needs now, but in the future, and selecting that talent for the right position within the organization; and
2.   Develop talent through using of proper assessment tools, arranging experience to provide knowledge, coaching the individual and providing feedback to ensure learning occurs; then
3.   Retain talent through recognition programs, employing encouragement and providing rewards. (Rothwell, 2005, p. 389)

The increasing interconnectivity and mobility of the workforce means that competition for the best leaders will become increasingly intense. "One way to ensure that you have the right people in the right jobs in this rapidly shifting environment is by writing job descriptions for the kind of people you need in each job as it will exist tomorrow, then match those descriptions against the talents and abilities of the people holding those jobs today" (Bossidy & Charan, 2009, p. xvi). This out-year perspective is important as the leader predicts the type of leadership the organization will need as it contemplates navigation of the uncharted waters of the future environment. As such, the leader must "begin now to cultivate the leaders of the future, testing and evaluating people for their ability to execute in the face of new challenges and circumstances" (Bossidy & Charan, 2009, p. xvi).

Unlike tangible assets (e.g., financial, equipment, technology, etc.), the intangible asset of *knowledge*—such as gained by developing talent—actually *increases as it is applied*. Put succinctly, the organization becomes smarter. Scholars have found "human capital does not depreciate in value as it is used" (Hitt et al., 2009, p. 11). If future leaders could be taught "to think of themselves less as heroes and more as people who face difficult decisions, and to recognize the tradeoffs involved in making those choices, we will be more likely to see them ask for help from others" (Khurana, 2002, p. 215). We saw this characteristic described previously with the quote, "it's loving yourself enough to get out of the way so other people can be magnificent" (Blanchard & Barrett, 2011, p. 22). By asking others for assistance when required, a learning environment is encouraged, which increases corporate knowledge and expertise. Employees will understand that it is "OK to ask for help, since the CEO is doing it." This has the potential for reducing their fears, increasing their trust, and, as a bi-product, increasing their learning. All of these results are superb for organizations operating within a contested environment.

We see that, "in a global knowledge economy, expertise is often the key to competitive advantage" (Rothwell, 2010, p. 52). This intangible advantage, knowledge and expertise, is unique to each organization, similar to the fingerprints on a person's hand. And, like fingerprints, an organization's knowledge and experience cannot be exactly copied. If the organization sought competitive advantage through tangible assets, such as technology, there is a risk that others could duplicate the technology. "Little of technology is proprietary" (Pfeffer, 1994, p. 12). However, those fingerprints found in the organization's knowledge and experiences are unique and could be "game changers" in a competitive environment.

Through the incorporation of succession planning, three very important goals may be achieved. "First, the plan would contribute to the overall strategic business plan; second, by considering replacement needs, the organization would facilitate employee training, education and development;

third, the talent pool of promotable employees would be increased" (Rothwell, 2005, pp. 20-24). Succession planning fully supports the concept of treating employees as hired hearts instead of merely hired hands. It demonstrates that leadership places value in the continuing education of its employees and within a globally free, ever-changing environment, by attracting, developing and retaining talent through succession planning, the organization is best prepared to compete. "Succession planning is more than selecting someone with an appropriate skill set—it's about finding someone who is in lockstep with the original cause around which the company was founded. That's why we call it succession, not replacement" (Sinek, 2011, p. 201). Put together, a lasting legacy that survives the incumbent CEO is more likely. Within the next chapter, we will explore the idea of the "cause," or in our vernacular, "purpose," but suffice it to say, "when the person who personifies the why [purpose] departs without clearly articulating why the company was founded in the first place, they leave no clear cause [purpose] for their successor to lead" (Sinek, 2011, p. 197).

Rest—A Technique that Averts Burnout

As leaders of today strive to achieve a lasting legacy, or even to make ends meet, they may feel as a lit candle, with its flame being smothered. Perhaps there is a feeling of being just as tired preparing for work in the morning as one felt the night before. There might be a sense that productivity is waning, along with increased stresses on the job. These, and many more characteristics may be indicators of potential burnout. But leaders (and followers) can take heart. Their salvation may be found in the simple act of personal Sabbaths, which allow for rest and renewal. A leader's understanding of their personal burnout symptoms, as well as their employees' symptoms and the implied need for rest is another aspect leaders should see clearly so as to be consistent with the idea of viewing people as hired hearts.

The pressures for employees, and especially leaders within the global marketplace, are increasing daily. This environment, with rapidly increasing technology, mobility, and inter-connectedness, demands "working harder, faster, and with higher quality to survive" (Carr & Tang, 2005, p. 161). Rightly or wrongly, the leader is placed in a position where, "to a great extent, the executive is the lightning rod for blame however complex the causes of success and failure may be" (Delbecq & Friedlander, 1995, p. 263). It is increasingly easy for leaders to become overwhelmed, being "seduced by promises of more: more money, more recognition, more satisfaction, more information…even when our intentions are noble and our efforts sincere" (Muller, 1999, p. 14). Leaders may find themselves needing to portray an image of optimism and energy, even when, perhaps, feeling run down. A typical day may include:

- Intelligence gathering and complex problem solving regarding the organization's strategy;
- Frequent random contacts and personal visibility in the work spaces, which demand active listening and tactical problem solving;
- Delicate conversations with emergent leaders, unsatisfied coalitions with a variety of petitions and grievances;
- Constant attention to selection of key players; and
- Symbolic events in which the executive must be upbeat and convey energy and optimism in the face of daunting organizational challenges (Delbecq & Friedlander, 1995, p. 263).

That typical day is compounded by a work schedule that often exceeds a 60-hour workweek. Like the proverbial captain of a ship, leaders may find themselves to be the first in and the last to leave. Lunch, if taken, might be a working meal. "In the relentless busyness of modern life, [the leader may have] lost the rhythm between work and rest" (Muller, 1999, p. 14). This could result in burnout, the smothering of the leader's flame, and "winning at work may mean losing at life…[because] in a human life, success cannot be sustained over the long term by denying the existence of problems" (O'Neil, 2004, p. 14). These problems "may have nothing to do with finding the best locations, computer systems, or product manager, but with deeply personal matters such as the loss of passion, commitment, vision, and meaning" (O'Neil, 2004, p. 14). The result for whoever is so afflicted, and especially the leader, is burnout.

Burnout implies "that once a fire was burning but the fire cannot continue burning brightly unless there are sufficient resources that keep being replenished" (Schaufeli, Leiter, & Maslach, 2009, p. 205). Where once there was intense involvement that resulted in meaningful impact, there is now exhaustion. Major sources of burnout are: 1) work overload; 2) lack of control; 3) insufficient reward; 4) unfairness in the system; 5) breakdown of community; and 6) value conflict (Maslach & Leiter, 1997, p. 26). This can result in a person feeling "tired, unfulfilled, powerless, or frustrated" (Ammondson, 2001, p. 68), and again, it is not solely a leadership phenomenon, meaning followers can and do experience the same things.

As the corporate leader surveys leaders at lower tiers within the organization, there may be patterns of "low productivity, depressed morale, and high turnover of valuable employees who possess specialized knowledge and skills. High rates of employee burnout also can increase the likelihood of workplace violence" (Carr & Tang, 2005, p. 162). Burnout can be a situation that affects individuals throughout the organization, and eventually will have negative results on the "bottom line." But there is a way for all to find relief…simply, rest!

It may come as a surprise to the leader that "the act of resting is a holy act" (Wuellner, 1998, p. 122). However, the concept of rest runs counter to our culture. Western culture "supposes that action and accomplishment are better than rest, that doing something—anything—is better than doing nothing" (Muller, 1999, p. 14). But we are challenged in the Book of Exodus to *remember*: "Remember the Sabbath" (Exodus 20:8, NIV), we are told. This implies that though we once knew this, we have forgotten, and surely due to our busyness, and lack of desire to rest, perhaps we have. It is also a means of seeing the past in a clear manner! How often as parents do we admonish busy children to take a nap, during the day, yet as adults we seem to forget this need for rest. Perhaps this basic thought is why we are told to remember. This idea of resting was modeled for all of us, leaders included, within the opening sections of the first book of the Bible: "on the seventh day God finished His work which He had done, and He rested" (Genesis 2:2, ASV). Additionally, scholars have noted that we should provide ourselves with mini-Sabbaticals, which is also on display in the Creation narrative:

At every juncture God acts, steps back, and rests. God invokes the light, separates it from the darkness…and steps back. *And God saw that it was good*. Then God makes a place for heaven and earth, separates the sea from dry land…and steps back. *And God saw that it was good.* (Muller, 1999, p. 55)

This act of "seeing that it was good" implies a break in the action…taking time to assess…resting. Rest is not only a holy act; it also provides clarity of thought. "Weariness [the absence of rest], can make us seek gratification and energy from food or drugs, or from egoistic postures" (Willard, 2002, p. 176). At least one scholar recommends tiny Sabbaths each hour, then an hour each day, then a day each week, and also at least a week each year (Wuellner, 1998, pp. 121-122). The point behind these Sabbath periods is to obtain inner renewal, done with joy, not compulsion.

A sample listing of strategies to achieve rest from our exhausted lives includes:
• *Value your sleep.* Proper sleep aids in concentration and bolsters the immune system.
• *Take a seven-minute revitalization break* (Ammondson, 2001, p. 69). This provides an opportunity to commune with nature, while letting the stresses from your leadership position fade away, if only for seven minutes. Those breaks may allow you to "see what no one else is seeing, having a perspective that no one else has taken" (Michalko, 2001, p. 8), which could lead to innovation and creativity breakthroughs.
• *Make home your sanctuary.* "Home is a place for personal rest, renewal, and family activity. Work is not brought home. Weekends are sacred and preserved for family" (Delbecq & Friedlander, 1995, p. 264). This can be quite a challenge. As I write this text, I have already put in a long day (typically consisting of more than 9 hours of work with lunch at my desk), and am now writing this piece at home. But I realize this is just a season, and when it is complete, I will seek rest, which is the salient point here. Seek opportunities to make home a safe haven, a fortress of solitude away from your daily work-related troubles, while realizing that there may be seasons in your life where bringing work home is essential.
• *Evaluate and prioritize your work* by keeping a daily log, and learn to say "no."
• *Plan a getaway.* "Get away from life's fast pace for a weekend or even a day. Pick a quiet, nurturing environment where you can rest…unplug the phone, [turn off your electronic devices], and recharge your batteries (Ammondson, 2001, p. 69). We live in a period of time where being disconnected is increasingly challenging, and sadly, we seem to relish our ability to be connected, even at inappropriate times (such as while driving a vehicle). Portable electronic devices enable us to be in touch or connected even when we should be resting. Now, all of us, but especially leaders, must work at being disconnected during certain periods. By the same token, leaders should think hard about sending that message for "urgent" work to a subordinate during times the subordinate should be sleeping, or at least not at work! Everyone understands a crisis, but every hour of every day cannot be a crisis.

There are many demands facing corporate leadership, all requiring high attention and high energy. It may be possible to maintain peak attention and energy for a while, but there will come a point when burnout may result. The recommendations presented reinforce the point that though one may be the leader, the leader is not indispensable and is of limited value to the organization if the abilities for which the leader is hired are worn down. Work is only one aspect of the leader's life, and a proper balance between work and rest should be sought. The Sabbath is indeed a gift—an essential gift worth remembering for effective leadership. The leader must see this clearly, not only for himself, but also for his followers.

I will close this portion with a lengthy quotation from Gordon Bethune. Bethune was the CEO of Continental Airlines from 1994-2004. At the time he took over, Continental had faced bankruptcy twice and was headed in that direction again. As Bethune saw it, "we were going nowhere like we had an appointment" (Bethune & Huler, 1998, p. 3). It was ranked last in virtually every measurable performance category, however, "it was soon ranked as one of the best companies to work for in America" (Sinek, 2011, p. 84). Bethune's predecessor had an issue with trust: "Frank Lorenzo would not even drink a soda on a Continental plane if he didn't open the can himself…the executive floor was off-limits to most people…the suites were locked…no one trusted him" (Sinek, 2011, p. 85). "On October 24, 1994, I [Bethune] did a very significant thing in the executive suite of Continental Airlines…I opened the doors" (Bethune & Huler, 1998, p. 3). Bethune's own words provide a stark contrast to what he saw that first day:

Business is people. That's it. You need to know about the business you're running; you need to know how to do your job. But whatever you're doing, and whatever kind of manager you are, everything you do is really just creating, developing, and maintaining good, healthy, honest and straightforward relationships. Forget it for a second and something will remind you. Forget it for a month and your profits will fall. Forget if for a year and your company will stagger. Forget if for much more than that and you'll be going down for the third time—and you'd better hope somebody shows up to save your bacon. (Bethune & Huler, 1998, p. 278)

Chapter Summary

- Successful leaders clearly see others in their organization as hired hearts, not as commodities. They demonstrate this by loving those in their employ.
- Trust is a result of love, and trust inspires confidence, mitigates fear, and opens the door for creativity.
- Communication is the tool we use to communicate, and there are cultural concerns affecting how we are oriented, even for non-verbal communication that the leader must see clearly, to effectively influence others.
- Succession planning, as a process, is essential for the long-term health of an organization, where talent will be developed to meet present-day and future organizational requirements. Succession planning demonstrates that leadership cares about the individuals and their growth in the organization.
- To avert potential burnout, which may result in loss of productivity, rest is the only antidote.

Questions to Ponder

1. Considering attributes of love as: patience, kindness, without envy, not boastful, not conceited, acting properly, not selfish, not provoked, not keeping record of wrongs, finding no joy in unrighteousness, and rejoicing in truth, when do you demonstrate each of these attributes?
2. Thinking about the above attributes, when do you struggle to demonstrate each?
3. What are you, as the leader, doing to establish and nurture a desired culture within your organization?

Chapter 4

PURPOSE—WHAT IS YOUR QUEST? ARE YOU ORGANIZED TO ACHIEVE IT?

"Would you tell me, please, which way I ought to go from here?"
"That depends a good deal on where you want to get to," said the Cat.
"I don't much care where—" said Alice.
"Then it doesn't matter which way you go," said the Cat.
"—so long as I get somewhere," Alice added as an explanation.
"Oh, you're sure to do that," said the Cat, "if you only walk long enough."
(Carroll, 1920, p. 89)

--

You and these people who come to you will only wear yourselves out. The work is too heavy for you; you cannot handle it alone. Listen now to me and I will give you some advice, and may God be with you. You must be the people's representative before God and bring their disputes to Him. Teach them His decrees and instructions, and show them the way they are to live and how they are to behave. But select capable men from all the people—men who fear God, trustworthy men who hate dishonest gain—and appoint them as officials over thousands, hundreds, fifties and tens. Have them serve as judges for the people at all times, but have them bring every difficult case to you; the simple cases they can decide themselves. That will make your load lighter because they will share it with you.
(Exodus 18: 18-22)

This chapter, dealing with purpose, marks the third and final leg of the SC triad. It presupposes the preceding legs are clear to the leader. There seems to be a human condition where one wrestles with purpose, attempting to understand "why" in a general sense. "Man's search for meaning is the primary motivation in his life and not a 'secondary rationalization' of instinctual drives. Man…is able to live and even to die for the sake of his ideals and values" (Frankl, 2006, p. 99). We need to know where we are going and why, otherwise it really does not matter which road we take. This point was made clear to Alice by the Cheshire Cat in Lewis Carroll's *Alice's Adventures in Wonderland*. This truth, on an individual level, applies equally to organizations. Further, organizations need to be totally in alignment with that purpose, as Moses' father-in-law, Jethro, advised in the second example. These two major concepts are the thrust of this chapter.

While researching for this work, I was asked to eulogize my 15-year-old daughter at her high school. I offer those words at this juncture:

Just last week (Memorial Day) our nation took the time to remember Americans who gave their lives so that you and I could have freedoms so many take for granted. Whether it was during the Civil War or the War against Terror, though their losses were tragic and sometimes shattered the families from which they came, there was at least a purpose behind their loss. The Bible tells us,

"Greater love has no one than this, that one lay down his life for his friends." Today, though we may grieve for those Americans, we can have some comfort for those warriors…but, how do I as Julia's father find ANY comfort in her senseless loss of life due to a driver not paying attention? She entered the world ready to go, starting to breathe even before fully birthed, which created some breathing problems for her. Her little body was hooked to a huge amount of tubes and wires, and we were not even able to bring her home for quite some time. For the next 15 years she grew into a lovely and loving young lady. I have always been amazed at what I've been able to learn from her! She loved nature, music, the Grafton Band, and mostly, Jesus. She was truly a blessing to her mother and I, and everyone she touched.

Now, I am left without the ability to hug her before she goes to bed. I can't teach her to drive, nor can I listen to her practicing her music or dancing. I can't give her prom date specific instructions on how I want him to present himself…I won't be able to do the father-daughter dance at her wedding…and for what? The picture that remains in my mind is of her lifeless body. I can't seem to shake it, and I am struggling to not become very angry.

Of course, my wife and I are not alone in our grief. As we lost Julia, so too did Tony's family. Josie will have physical and emotional scars that will last her lifetime; and Emmerson, well, because of a misprioritized [sic] moment, his entire future is ruined. Whatever hopes and dreams he had are probably as dead as Julia and Tony. Even worse, the memory of what happened will stick with him for the rest of his life. So, in many ways, he too died in that crash. Four young lives, many families and friends all were devastated in an instant of time.

So maybe you didn't know our Julia Myntrue Victoria Hoyes. Maybe you didn't have a chance to experience her sweetness and her love of life. Perhaps you did not know Tony, or Josie, or Emmerson. But, my hope and prayer for every single one of us in this room is that their lives, like those of our nation's heroes that we remembered on Memorial Day, will not have been in vain. That behind this seemingly senseless disaster, there will be some good, that perhaps you and I will think very hard about what we are doing when we get behind the wheel of a car, and in that way, other lives might be saved.

I used to fly fighter aircraft in the USAF. There is one rule that is drilled into us right from the beginning of our flight training: Aviate, Navigate, Communicate. That's the sequence of importance. Aviate, Navigate, Communicate. First, you ensure you are in control of your aircraft (which includes knowing what other aircraft around you are doing), next, know where you are and where you want to go, and only then, do you communicate with others. That same principal holds true whether things are routine, in an emergency situation or in combat. I want to offer that same principle to all of us when behind the wheel of a car. Operate, navigate, communicate. When you or I get behind the wheel of a car, our first and primary focus should be on operating that vehicle in a safe manner. Nothing else matters as much as that. Nothing else matters. So, I'd like you all to say that with me: OPERATE, NAVIGATE, COMMUNICATE.

I'd like us to remember the lives of Emmerson, Tony, Josie and Julia, and also that OPERATE is the main priority when driving. Perhaps if we did that, there would be some purpose for this tragedy, and, in a way, those four young people provided ultimate love for us all, by laying down their lives for all of us. (M. Hoyes, 2014)

Thankfully, that speech was part of a "3D—Driving Drunk Distracted" Drivers Education Program, devised by the York County Sheriff's Office and other county agencies. Within that scenario, my daughter was filmed as the deceased victim of a vehicular accident. The scenario included such events as on-the-scene paramedic, police and fire department support, parental notification of the accident, flight for life, and a gathering of the entire student body in the auditorium to view the eulogy. The important thing to note from that speech is the search for a reason or a purpose…we seek to understand why something happened when a tragedy arises. In a like manner, we also perform better when we understand why, when what we are doing makes sense, particularly if the feeling reaches the level of a passion. Leadership, as we have already stated, is a "process whereby an individual influences a group of individuals to achieve a *common goal*" (Northouse, 2010, p. 3). This common goal is our purpose. As a further motivator, this idea of understanding purpose is essential for long-term organizational health and success, as the idea of purpose or passion may also be called a "calling" in this context:

Research has shown that people who do the same work can view it as a job, a career, or a calling, and that people who view their work as a calling find more satisfaction and do better work than people with the other two orientations. Callings have several characteristics, but one significant factor that distinguishes them from jobs and careers is the relative insignificance of instrumental factors to why people are working in the first place. Instead, callings denote a focus on the fulfillment experienced from the work itself, often accompanied by a sense that the work contributes to others in a meaningful way. Finding ways to emphasize the internal and minimize the instrumental may lead to better and more satisfied students and soldiers. (Wrzesniewski, Schwartz, Cong, Kane, Omar, & Kolditz, 2014, p. 5)

Purpose Matters…Greatly!

Let us step back in time roughly five hundred years. We find ourselves in Rome, Italy, and Michelangelo Buonarroti, known today simply as Michelangelo, had this to say:

I've grown a goitre by dwelling in this den —
As cats from stagnant streams in Lombardy,
Or in what other land they hap to be —
Which drives the belly close beneath the chin:
My beard turns up to heaven; my nape falls in
Fixed on my spine: my breast-bone visibly
Grows like a harp: a rich embroidery
Bedews my face from brush-drips, thick and thin.
My loins into my paunch like levers grind:
My buttock like a crupper bears my weight;
My feet unguided wander to and fro;
In front my skin grows loose and long; behind,
By bending it becomes more taut and strait;

Crosswise I strain me like a Syrian bow:
Whence false and quaint, I know,
Must be the fruit of squinting brain and eye;
For ill can aim the gun that bends awry.

Come then, Giovanni, try
To succour my dead pictures and my fame;
Since foul I fare and painting is my shame. (Michelangelo, n.d.)

The artist's words within the above sonnet indicate the personal agony Michelangelo must have felt as he finished painting the ceiling of the Sistine Chapel over a period of four years. It is debated whether he accomplished that major work on scaffolding hundreds of feet in the air while lying down, or whether he was standing up. Likewise, some hold that Michelangelo "had assembled a team of thirteen artists to help complete the work" (Burkus, 2014, p. 110). Whether he was on his back, standing, or had a team of assistants, the point is that the creative responsibility was his. He was the leader of the effort, whether leading solely himself under contract from Pope Julius II, or a team of others. "To any visitor of Michelangelo's Sistine Chapel, two features become immediately and undeniably apparent: 1) the ceiling is really high up, and 2) there are a lot of paintings up there" (Zappella, n.d.). Perhaps, in the context of this discussion, there is a third feature that may be discerned: Michelangelo had a clear purpose driving him (and perhaps those he engaged for assistance). And now, over five hundred years later, millions of visitors to the Sistine Chapel are able to partake in his purpose, his vision.

Let us advance ourselves in time a bit and look at a more current example, one concerning two stonemasons, who are working at the same project site:

You walk up to the first stonemason and ask, "Do you like your job?" He looks up at you and replies, "I've been building this wall for as long as I can remember. The work is monotonous…but it's a job. It pays the bills." About thirty feet away, you walk up to a second stonemason. You ask him the same question…He looks up and replies, "I love my job. I'm building a cathedral. The stones are heavy and lifting them day after day can be backbreaking. I'm not even sure if this project will be completed in my lifetime. But I'm building a cathedral." (Sinek, 2011, p. 95)

The first stonemason may be doing an adequate, even satisfactory job, but the second is giving his heart. The first stonemason may leave that job for an organization offering more pay, but the second considers himself to be part of a mission, or a purpose and, for that reason, may not accept a higher paying job. The second stonemason may be more inclined to offer innovations to a foreman or supervisor, to enable increased efficiency in the attainment of the purpose, the former is likely to keep his mouth and his mind closed. The first may feel some degree of animosity towards those he perceives as having a cushier task, whereas the second does not see himself as more or less important than anyone else, because they are all doing their parts to build that cathedral. The second stonemason understands the purpose for why he is there and why the organization exists while the former did not.

The above example provides an internal perspective. How might we visualize this same approach when dealing with an external customer? Perhaps you are in the sales business with a product you'd like your customer to purchase. You have two sales employees for your printing business, and their dialogue with prospective customers proceeds as follows:

Salesperson A: "We prep. We print. We bind. We mail." Salesperson B: "Everything we do is focused on making you look good and driving better results. Print is how we do it. Now, let me tell you about our capabilities." Which one do you think sells more? (Tedesco & Farquhason, 2012, p. 67)

The stonemasons or the salespersons in the above examples probably did not create their inclinations. Rather the leader potentially influenced them, failing with the former, succeeding with the latter. Recall from our previous discussion that leadership is the process of influencing, and influencing occurs when the leader communicates. Bethune explains Continental's approach as follows:

We made sure every employee in the organization understood that the Go Forward Plan was our blueprint—and why. Greg Brenneman and I and other top-level managers spread the word on the Go Forward Plan throughout the company. In meetings at virtually every site in the company we introduced employees to the plan, explaining how it addressed not just some but all of Continental's problems. (Bethune & Huler, 1998, p. 39)

When we speak of purpose, we must understand that it is not a plan. On the steps of the Lincoln Memorial on a hot summer day in August 1963, a 34-year-old Dr. Martin Luther King Jr. addressed over 250,000 people who were present. Those people had assembled peacefully in what, at that time, was the largest gathering of protesters in Washington D.C. history. Over, and over, and over again, during his 17-minute speech, Dr. King implored those in attendance to clearly see his dream. "That speech was what he believed, not how they were going to do it. He gave the 'I Have a Dream' speech, not the 'I Have a Plan' speech. It was a statement of purpose and not a comprehensive 12-point plan" (Sinek, 2011, p. 129). The intention of that speech was to not only influence, but to also inspire others to take action. Its aim was to touch the heart of the listener, perhaps evoking the sense of a calling to achieve Dr. King's vision. How does vision relate to purpose? A useful way to distinguish between the two is: "Our visions are the world we imagine, the tangible results of what the world would look like if we spent every day in pursuit of our why [purpose]" (Sinek, 2011, p. 228). We have seen from these examples that purpose matters!

If you, as the leader, can translate your organization's reason for being into a purpose or why statement "it is easier for all employees to stay on the same page" (Tedesco & Farquhason, 2012, p. 67), and it is also easier for customers to understand you. This enables your organization to better form a relationship with that customer, which promotes loyalty. They are more likely to buy what you're selling rather than shopping around for a better deal. Understanding the purpose internally and externally presents long-term, consistent value for the organization. We will see an example of this in a later chapter, but let's look briefly at Apple. "Apple has long infused their "why" [purpose] statement—'Think Different'—into everything they've done. Yes, they started as a computer company, but that soon became almost an afterthought" (Tedesco & Farquhason, 2012, p. 68).

If your organization does not understand its purpose, it is doubtful potential customers will either. "When railroads first began crisscrossing the United States in the 19th century, they were the ideal form of transportation: fast, inexpensive, solid, flexible, and expansive" (Gryskiewicz, 1999, p. 116). Then, competition arose from automobiles and air travel. But was that the real issue that resulted in the lack of growth for railroads? Scholars believe the reason was because the railroad industry failed to understand their purpose, or at a minimum, they had a misplaced purpose:

> The railroads did not stop growing because the need for passenger and freight transportation declined. That grew. The railroads are in trouble today not because the need was filled by others (cars, trucks, airplanes, even telephones), but because it was not filled by the railroads themselves. They let others take customers away from them because they assumed themselves to be in the railroad business rather than in the transportation business. (Levitt, 1975, p. 1)

Let us briefly look at a contrasting approach, where the organization's purpose is understood and the effect it has on its business. According to Richard Branson, chair of Virgin Group of Companies, "We didn't want to get in the transportation industry; we're still in the entertainment industry—at 25,000 feet" (Gryskiewicz, 1999, p. 19). By clearly seeing their purpose as entertainment that just happens to be at altitude, Virgin Atlantic Airlines, "in 2012 carried 5.4 million passengers, making it the seventh-largest airline in the United Kingdom, in terms of passenger volume" ("All services," 2012). What does that purpose look like? "Virgin has magicians and masseuses and videos at each seat on many of its flights, and Range Rover limousine service at Heathrow Airport provides an extension of service beyond the airport" (Gryskiewicz, 1999, p. 19). Some may view these examples as gimmicks, however, they demonstrate a clear view of the purpose, as well as an effort to organize that is aligned with that purpose. We will address this aspect of organizational alignment to purpose later in this chapter.

How much does the quest for purpose, why, or meaning matter? Victor Frankl pens a narrative about his experiences in a Nazi prison camp in his book, *Man's Search for Meaning*. Miraculously, Frankl survived his imprisonment to author that book; but the book is not solely about his experiences in a concentration camp as it is the sources of the strength he and others had to survive in that environment. He quotes Nietzsche, writing: "He who has a Why [sic] to live for can bear almost any How [sic]" (Frankl, 2006, p. ix). The why, or purpose, gave those prisoners a reason to live and not give up, even when facing likely death. He writes, "Man is that being who invented the gas chambers of Auschwitz; however, he is also that being who entered those gas chambers upright, with the Lord's Prayer of the *Sherma Yisrael* on his lips" (Frankl, 2006, p. xii). Purpose matters. It matters greatly on an individual level as well as on an organizational one. Imagine an organization led by those who realize, "Man…is able to live and even to die for the sake of his ideals and values" (Frankl, 2006, p. 99), and that leader is able to hire, educate, retain, and promote workers who embody the values of the organization's leadership. This is the area we will explore next as we prepare to conclude this work, but as we do so, bear in mind and never lose sight: purpose matters greatly.

Purpose and Organizational Design

There are six elements we will concern ourselves with through this discussion of organizational design and its relationship to purpose. Those elements are: the environment, strategy, structure, processes, rewards, and people. As we discuss each of these elements, the reader must see clearly their relationship to the leadership triad of principles, people and purpose. Admittedly, "people" appears within both the triad of this SC discussion as well as an element of purpose. We use the word "model" to describe a system that may be followed in this context, which will be metaphorically described as a star. We are mindful that "the use of metaphor implies a way of thinking and a way of seeing that pervades how we understand our world" (Morgan, 2006, p. 4), however, we must remain alert for the dangers in using them. "Metaphor is inherently paradoxical. It can create powerful insights that also become distortions, as the way of seeing created through a metaphor becomes a way of not seeing" (Morgan, 2006, p. 5). The same is true for our mental models in general:

> Mental models are deeply ingrained assumptions, generalizations, or even pictures or images that influence how we understand the world and how we take action. Very often, we are not consciously aware of our mental models or the effects they have on our behavior. (Senge, 2006, p. 8)

As this work hopes to provide the reader with the understanding, desire and means to see clearly, we must tread this ground of discussing models and metaphors rather carefully. We need to be careful that we do not make assumptions that impede our ability to see clearly. As leaders, we also need to communicate to our organization so that they do not make faulty assumptions either. Also, as leaders, we must be certain that our actions coincide with our words.

Jay Galbraith, an internationally recognized expert on organization design, presents the reader with his star model as a metaphor for understanding organizational design in his book, "*Designing organizations: An executive guide to strategy, structure, and process.*" The intention of this chapter is to provide the reader with an understanding of an augmented view of Galbraith's model, which may be employed within the reader's organization. Whether or not an organization is categorized as federal or shamrock (Handy, 1989), boundaryless (Ashkenas et al., 2002), flexible (Overholt, 1997), star (Galbraith, 2002), or any of the countless models devised, leaders will continue to face questions concerning organizational design, particularly as that design relates to the organization's purpose.

Though we will use Galbraith's model as an entry point, we also understand that different environments require different relationships for optimum effectiveness (Davis, 1973, p. 3). Galbraith concludes, "any organizational model can be effective in the right circumstances and for the right company" (Galbraith, 2002, p. 180). What these authors are cautioning, and what this author believes, is that there is no singular organizational design that will work for all situations, cultures, or company. However, the approach presented provides a framework for discussing not only the impact of the environment on organizational design, but also how the design must align with the company's purpose.

As we consider the phrase "organizational design," we are not making a leap to the whiteboard to craft a hierarchy scheme that traces the CEO through all levels of the organization. Keidel (1995) purports, "scores of managers are convinced that design equals structure equals organizational chart and that changing design amounts to little more than altering boxes and lines" (p. 7). This is not where we are going with our discussion in the slightest. On the contrary, due to our focus on the leader and her relationship to the organization and the environment, we see organizational design as "the purposeful specification of relationships" (Keidel, 1995, p. 6).

Figure 2. Galbraith's Star Model and its Augmentation

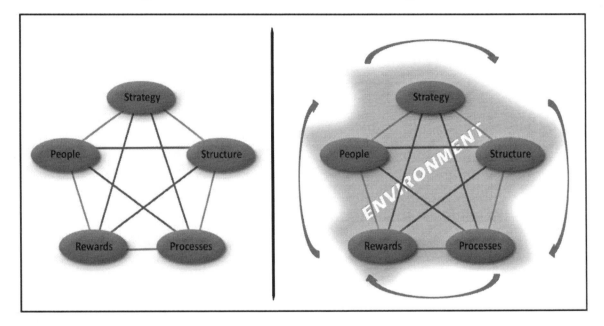

[Adapted from: Galbraith, J. R. (2002). *Designing organizations:*
An executive guide to strategy, structure, and process, **and Hoyes, M. B. (2012).**
*Organizational design: Revisiting Galbraith's star model.***]**

Figure 2 depicts Galbraith's Star Model, as well as the proposed augmented or enhanced version of his model for comparison. As an overview, this work stipulates that environment is a factor in each of the five elements, but it also will be discussed by itself. The model is cyclic, meaning that due to changing factors in the environment, and perhaps some of the elements, there may be tweaks required to the organization's design over time (Hoyes, 2012). As with Galbraith's original model, consisting of strategy, structure, processes, rewards, and people, each element must be in alignment with the others for the organization to succeed. This includes their relationship with the environment. Leaders must clearly see this interaction with the environment as they establish their organization's purpose and its design to fulfill that purpose. We continue to remember that *the organization exists to do something,* and the leader is responsible for articulating that purpose to achieve agreement from followers to accomplish that purpose.

Imagine the Butterfly Effect, that of a butterfly flapping its wings in Asia and causing a hurricane in the Atlantic (Sanders, 1998). This is a metaphor for how small changes or events can create complex results. This is what we are experiencing in a post-industrial world. This phenomenon, evidenced by technological innovations, led organizational designers to imagine organizations in more of an organic or biological sense, as they viewed the social and relational attributes of the organization. The objective in designing an organic unit is to leave the system open to the environment in order to make the most of new opportunities (McCaskey, 1974). The star model allows the leader to select a mechanistic, organic or a hybrid of the two techniques, which makes it quite powerful.

Environment

From birth, we wrestle with our environment. The newborn cries because she is hungry, hot, hurt, cold, wet, dry, or just because. All are attempts to deal with the environment. The 21st century presents a somewhat uncertain world, and in that world, some scholars see the most important business development as pursuing competitive advantage through new approaches to organization design (Nadler & Tushman, 1999). Due to the rapid pace of change, perhaps we find ourselves leaping before we look, without clearly understanding the environment in which we find ourselves a part. Sometimes the changes are subtle. Recall that "learning to see slow, gradual processes requires slowing down our frenetic pace and paying attention to the subtle as well as the dramatic" (Senge, 2006, p. 23). Contingency theory leads to the notion that organizations are most effective when their design characteristics match, or are contingent with their environment. When we view this post-Cold War environment, what do we see? How uncertain is the environment in which organizations operate?

Every time we purchase gasoline, whether at the pump for our cars or for our homes, we feel the effects of a global economy, where Wall Street, Main Street and you and I feel the shooting pains of economic decisions made across the globe. The Butterfly Effect, previously referenced, is felt in many domains. And, as we addressed earlier, we are more connected politically and economically than ever before. This connection is coupled with our full immersion in the Information Age. We are doing more things with portable telephones, tablet computers and the like, than previously imaginable. With stunning speed, the Internet is profoundly changing the way we work, go to school, shop, do business, and communicate (Nadler & Tushman, 1999). In addition to creating a better-informed and discriminating consumer, the economy is "shifting from one based on manufacturing to one that puts great value on information, services, support and distribution" (Nadler & Tushman, 1999, p. 48). Additionally, there is a premium value for speed of delivery.

As we have discussed, when operating in the global space, national culture is another factor worth considering. Recalling our earlier description in Chapter 3, power distance is reflecting inequality in power depending on prestige, influence, wealth, and status. High-power distance societies tend to use more coercive and referent power, whereas low-power distance societies use more legitimate power. Pondering again on the differences in national cultures, "on a scale from 0 to 100, the Swedish culture (31) is less hierarchical than the U.S. (40) and the Japanese (54) cultures" (Lillrank, Shani, & Lindberg, 2001). If the environment is one where the culture has a high power distance, there could be problems with authority relationships requiring employee input given to the structures that define communication and decision-making rules. High power distance implies a reluctance to provide the input you as the leader might seek. As the leader seeks to define the organization's purpose and align the organization's structure, she would have to keep in mind the potential cultural dispositions.

There will certainly be aspects of the environment that are unknown, and these unknowns can lead to crises the organization will have to deal with. Crises faced by organizations often have their roots in both the external and internal environments, and they are essentially bound to happen (Lin, Zhao, Ismail, & Carley, 2006). However, "the organization's capacity to understand its environment and to make the right kinds of strategic changes at the appropriate point in the cycle will determine its competitive strength" (Nadler & Tushman, 1999, p. 46). Two questions for the organization when crises arise are: How well is the organization's design capable of dealing with those crises? Will those crises derail the organization's alignment of its design to its purpose?

Strategy

T. Irene Sanders, a principal of Sanders & Company, states that strategic thinking, with its two major components of insight about the present and foresight about the future, is the centerpiece of strategic planning, and moreover, "is everyone's ongoing responsibility" (Sanders, 1998, p. 148). There are two important elements this brings forward, the first being that everyone has a role in strategic thinking. This fully supports what this text has espoused, and which we have implored leaders to see clearly. Second, we can gather that strategic thinking leads to strategic planning, or as Bonn states, "strategic planning is a process that should occur after strategic thinking" (Bonn, 2001, p. 64).

Strategic thinking is a "synthesizing process, using intuition and creativity" (Liedtka, 1998, p. 121), contrasted with strategic planning, which is an "analytical process aimed at programming already identified strategies. The outcome of strategic planning is a plan" (Liedtka, 1998, p. 121). From the individual's standpoint, strategic thinking requires time to acquire a holistic understanding of the environment, creativity brought about by generating ideas and a vision for the organization's role in the future state. Strategic visions are "picture[s] or images people carry in their heads and hearts" (Bonn, 2001, p. 66). To foster strategic thinking, an organization encourages "ongoing dialogue among the top team, and takes advantage of the ingenuity and creativity of every individual employee"(Bonn, 2001, p. 66). This builds what can be called a shared vision or shared purpose. "When there is a genuine shared vision (as opposed to the all-too-often familiar vision statement), people excel and learn, not because they are told to, but because they want to" (Senge, 2006, p. 9). The above comments highlight the interrelated nature of this element with the remaining elements of the augmented model, as well as the point we have already discussed. Throughout this undertaking, the organization's purpose must remain in focus.

The environment drives the strategic architecture of the enterprise. "It does this either through anticipation of or in reaction to, major changes in the marketplace" (Nadler & Tushman, 1999, p. 46). Strategy is the organization's formula for winning, consisting of its goals and objectives, its values, missions and basic direction. It delineates the products and services provided, markets served, value offered to the customer, and specifies the sources of competitive advantage, while striving to provide superior value (Galbraith, 2002, p. 10). As we have stated, strategy relies on strategic thinking, which has two major components: insight about the present and foresight about the future (Sanders, 1998, p. 152). Present and future what? The environment and the corporation's position within it! Hence, strategic thinking resulting in strategy development follows from a well-understood view of the environment as it was, is, and as it could be in the future. There are four questions that might be explored when developing a strategy:

1. What future do we want to create?
2. What system change is necessary for that future to become a reality?
3. Which leverage points in the system will move it in the desired direction?
4. How will we know when we're finished, and what is the exit plan? (Warden & Russell, 2002, p. 6)

Southwest Airlines prepares for the future by practicing the art of "what if…" using future scenario generation. "Future scenario generation is designed to periodically create future scenarios the company could face [asking, "what if?"], and it enables Southwest to prepare for the future in a way that provides direction for the company yet allows it to maneuver on many fronts. This reduces the likelihood that Southwest will get caught off guard" (Freiberg & Freiberg, 1997, p. 86), and establishes a formula designed to win. Once that formula for winning is clearly understood, it is then the leader who examines the structure of the organization, again, within the context of the environment (which is viewed from both an internal and external perspective).

Structure

Again, typically, when one discusses organizational design, structure is the entry point assumed. The whiteboard and markers are pulled out, and a new organizational hierarchy is charted. Interestingly, some scholars begin their discussions concerning organizational design by whipping out their whiteboards and markers also: "Organization design involves decisions about the configuration of the formal organizational arrangements, including formal structures, processes, and systems that make up an organization" (Nadler & Tushman, 1997, p. 48). However, we have seen, thus far, that there are certainly essential steps that precede this venture, and that they should not be taken for granted as having been accomplished. Assuming the leader can see the environment clearly, communicates well with his people, and is a person of principles, structure generally falls into four areas:

1. *Specialization* – the type and number of job specialties used to perform the work (Galbraith, 2002, p. 11). For example, companies in electronics, genetics and pharmaceuticals typically desire specialists who are able to push the limits of technology, whereas companies at the low- and medium-skill levels find their positions being automated or exported to developing countries. The determining environment for this is the type of industry in which the corporation is involved. If an organization is complex, they might also be characterized by a high degree of specialization. Here we see the interplay of both the internal and external environment regarding specialization. For example, NASA headquarters is organized so that particular departments are responsible for the performance of specialized activities, and because it specializes to more effectively cope with its environment, it becomes more differentiated or segmented (Hellreigel & Slocum Jr., 1973, p. 60). Of course, to safely

launch a technical marvel such as the now retired space shuttle, there must also be a high level of integration between the subsystems to accomplish that momentous task. So, in NASA's case, it would require an organizational design that enables it to have both a high degree of differentiation (or specialization) and a high degree of integration. This would enhance the ability of the craft to function in the hostile environment of space as well as navigate the precarious fiscal environment.

2. *Shape* – the number of people within the departments (span of control) at each level of the structure (Galbraith, 2002, p. 11). As we have already stated, today's environment demands increased speed. Organizations are increasingly structured wider and flatter than in previous years. This means there is less of a chain of command between the line worker and the CEO. This can result in fewer layers and quicker decision making, but larger span of control at each level. Each supervisor is responsible for more individuals.

3. *Distribution of power* – in its vertical dimension, it refers to centralization or decentralization (Galbraith, 2002, p. 11). In its lateral dimension, this is in reference to the movement of power to the department closest to the issues critical to the organization's mission (purpose). Again, to increase the organization's responsiveness (speed of delivery) to the customer, there is movement towards decentralization, which promotes decision-making power to those having direct customer interaction.

4. *Departmentalization* – basis for forming departments at each level, be they functions, products, workflow processes, markets or geography (Galbraith, 2002, p. 11). For example, "Boeing divides its design and manufacture of planes into product lines of narrow and wide bodies. However, the fabrication of major structural components is too expensive to duplicate for each line. They created a central fabrication unit, which includes all activities with requisite skills across product lines within that single unit" (Galbraith, 2002, p. 27). This is an example of a hybrid structure, and as the example depicts, is used due to the industry, the environment within which Boeing finds itself.

What should be abundantly clear from the above examples is the impact of the internal and external environment as structure is contemplated. The leader must see this relationship clearly and devise a structure that is in alignment with the organization's purpose and within the context of the environment. The structure must also be in alignment with the organization's strategy.

Processes

Management processes can either be vertical or horizontal. Vertical processes are typically business planning and budgeting processes, and allocate the scarce resources of funds and talent, while lateral or horizontal processes usually are designed around the work flow (Galbraith, 2002, p. 12). Companies must focus simultaneously on governments, customers, functions, vendors and products, all of the influencers in their environment. Lateral processes are designed to provide the company with the networks and capability of addressing these concerns, and is a decentralizing technique, which should also accelerate the decision process. Processes are how the information flows through the organization. Earlier, we saw that there may be informal and formal leadership executing that communication. Again, the better the understanding of the purpose, the better the communication efforts will be.

These processes should support and not run counter to the principles the organization holds dear, as well as the organization's purpose. For example, "At Southwest, every employee is a steward of the company's mission. If a policy or a practice appears to violate the intent of the company's mission or is inconsistent with its values, people are expected to speak up" (Freiberg & Freiberg, 1997, p. 130).

Rewards

The purpose of the reward element is to align employee goals with that of the organization (Galbraith, 2002, p. 12). Southwest airlines uses training (part of the people element below) as an essential motivating tool:

Employees are re-familiarized with the company's culture, mission statement, and corporate identity. Regular training prevents mistakes on the job, and new contacts are made. Because employees perceive that they are respected, valued and informed at all times, they tend to be more involved in the company and are more highly motivated. This, in turn, usually leads to higher performance. (Bunz & Maes, 1998, p. 165)

People

As we look at the five elements (six including the environment) and the need to clearly see an alignment of each to the other, the people element reflects similar traits as those we have already discussed. Here, the people element concerns human resource policies of recruiting, selection, rotation, training and development (Galbraith, 2002, p. 13). Though we touched on them earlier, some scholars see three forces that exist within the environment that increase the need for organizations to focus on people as the critical resource: global competition, labor shortages, and technological change (Overholt, Connally, Harrington, & Lopez, 2000, p. 38). Here we consider that the centers of economic activity will shift not just globally, but also regionally; the battlefield for talent will shift as we work not just globally but also instantaneously, and "corporate borders are becoming more blurred as interlinked 'ecosystems' of suppliers, producers and customers emerge" (Cohen, 2010, p. 4). Referring back to the power distance discussion, if the organizational design is focused on being highly centralized, the expected behavior would be that employees would only take action within specific guidelines, meaning they would typically defer decisions to superiors. Again, as we recall cultural dimensions, those cultures with a low hierarchical tolerance would see the demand for that hierarchical structure as a conflict. The impact of being a global corporation is that the organization's organizational design may need to be modified as the company expands to other cultures. As with the other elements of this model, author John Roberts concludes, "getting the people and culture aspects in alignment with the strategy (and the other elements) are typically more important for determining performance than fine tuning architectural routines...the cultural work is harder" (Bradley, 2006, p. 4).

Southwest Airlines' internal environment or culture de-emphasizes hierarchy, and encourages people to express their individuality, and the airline accepts failure as a natural and forgivable occurrence. Regarding hiring, Southwest hires on the basis of attitude. Herb Kelleher is famously quoted as stating: "If you don't have a good attitude, we don't want you, no matter how skilled you are. We can change skill level through training. We can't change attitude" (Bunz & Maes, 1998, p. 167).

Organizations, whose people policies are lacking, run the risk of creating organizational bystanders, defined as someone who fails to take necessary action when important threats—or opportunities—arise" (Gerstein & Shaw, 2008, p. 47). If an individual remains passive and a real threat is confirmed, there is a decreased likelihood of productive organizational outcomes, and the individual is a bystander. If the individual remains passive and it turns out there was no real threat, there is no cost to the individual, and that person could be viewed as a savvy professional who does not overreact. This individual is risk adverse, which may not be what the organization believes it espouses. Here are a few ideas to mitigate the likelihood of this bystander behavior:

1. Create mechanisms for expressing, and actively encouraging, dissenting points of view;
2. Ensure effective management systems that balance the need for short-term performance with the need for productive inquiry into potential threats;
3. Establish approaches to magnify and follow-up on near misses and other "weak signals";
4. Manage the impact of monolithic performance goals and budget cuts on the ability of individuals to surface and intervene in risky situations;
5. Formulate and practice contingency plans for disastrous, but low probability events;
6. Valuing robust, independent watchdogs; and
7. Establish relentless review, self-criticism, and a focus on learning at all levels, especially at the top. (Gerstein & Shaw, 2008, p. 47)

The leader must remember that it is through the people that the organization performs its mission. However, the organization, and its people do not operate in a vacuum. They impact and are impacted by the environment. Additionally, we have seen through this discussion why it is important for the elements to be in alignment with each other. But, the process we are describing does not end here.

Repeat

Surrounding the Augmented Star Model is a directional circle positioned to imply that the process is cyclic. Why? As we have stated from the outset, the environment is continuously changing, and what the leader and the organization may have planned due to foresight about the future, may not actually come to pass. The cyclic nature of the model ensures flexibility to meet the environment where it is. Additionally, there may be crisis events, which demand immediate thought and action. Some call this repetitive activity "continuous improvement." It offers the possibility of adaptation to changing requirements (in the environment) at the operative level of organizations and, simultaneously, affords a vehicle for meaningful employee participation (Lillrank et al., 2001, p. 42). Minor adjustments in organizational design are always being made during the life of an organization. The following could be viewed as typical reasons for those adjustments, occurring when:

1. Early in the life of an organization, most likely after the basic identity and strategy have been largely worked out; or

2. Significantly expanding or changing the organization's mission; or
3. Reorganizing. (Michael B McCaskey, 1974, p. 13)

Throughout this section we have made the case for the holistic view provided by the augmented version of the Galbraith Star model. We observed the interaction the environment makes on each of the elements, as well as the need for the elements to be in alignment with each other. The ability to understand the environment is a precursor to considering strategy, and must be considered throughout the life of the organization. As we conclude our discussion of purpose, we, as leaders, want to clearly see what our organization's purpose is, and how to best organize that organization to achieve that purpose. Both matter greatly, because unlike Alice, as we began this chapter, leaders must care about where their organization will get to.

Chapter Summary

- Leaders need to know where the organization is going and why, otherwise it really does not matter which road they take.
- The organization must be totally in alignment with its purpose (common goal).
- Leaders, through their influence, can affect the inclinations of their employees. Providing a common purpose is highly beneficial to the organization.
- The environment, strategy, structure, processes, rewards, and people form a useful model for thinking about the organization's design. Strategy, structure, processes, rewards and people must be in alignment with each other, and are impacted by the environment that exists (in contrast to the environment the organization seeks).

Questions to Ponder

1. Do the people in your organization know what will happen if they do an excellent job living out the purpose of the organization?
2. How is your internal customer service? How does it compare to your external customer service?
3. As a leader, what would people in your organization say you care about? Have you asked them this question? Do you know whether their answer is the same as what you say you care about?
4. What is the dominant culture within your organization, and what are you doing to create and nurture a desired culture?
5. As a leader, how do you respond to feedback? Do you even find yourself receiving feedback? If you never have received feedback, why do you think this is so?
6. How would you complete these sentences? "My company exists because _____. Our purpose is to _____. People should care because _____."
7. What is the nature of your organization's environment?
8. What type of strategy is being employed in your organization, and does it align with the organization's purpose?
9. How is your organization structured, and does that alignment facilitate the achievement of the organization's purpose?

Chapter 5

PRINCIPLES, PEOPLE, AND PURPOSE— SEEING CLEARLY AND SOUTHWEST AIRLINES

Let us put this concept of "seeing clearly: principles, people and purpose" together by a brief examination of a modern day success story. As we view the vignettes that follow, it is not my intention that they provide you with a blueprint for success as either a leader or for your organization. It should be clear by now; such a blueprint does not exist, for the DNA of your organization, when combined with the environment it finds itself in, is as unique as your own fingerprints. You must first metaphorically take the logs out of your own eyes to chart a successful path for yourself and your organization. Your environment, industry and organizational character or culture should determine the specific path you choose. As we examine the early period of this airline, there are abundant evidences of leadership's ability to clearly see principles, people and purpose as reflected in not only what they said, but also by their actions.

We recall: "Few large corporations live even half as long as a person. In 1983, a Royal Dutch/Shell study found that one-third of the firms that had been in the Fortune "500" in 1970 had vanished" (Senge, 2006, p. 17). So, it is quite appropriate that we examine Southwest Airlines, which had its inaugural flight on June 18, 1971. "Southwest is the only U.S. airline to earn a profit every year since 1973" (Freiberg & Freiberg, 1997, p. 4). This is inclusive of the years immediately following September 11, 2001. The company is presently ranked 160 in the Fortune 500 listing ("Southwest Airlines Co.," 2014). Table 5 depicts Southwest's steady improvement in the Fortune 500 rankings during the past 10 years. The environment the company finds itself operating within has certainly changed, yet they have prospered. For example, during that 40-plus-year period of Southwest Airlines' existence, the average price of gasoline has increased from under $0.50 per gallon to over $3.00, and yet they have been able to consistently turn a profit. There is nothing within what we have discussed that should suggest principles, people and purpose are not compatible with financial success—on the contrary, as Table 5 indicates!

Table 5. Ten-Year Look-back of Southwest Airlines' Fortune 500 Ranking

10-Year Southwest Airlines' Fortune 500 Ranking			
Year	Ranking	Year	Ranking
2014	160	2009	246
2013	164	2008	267
2012	167	2007	276
2011	205	2006	300
2010	229	2005	318

[Extracted from: Fortune Magazine – http://fortune.com/company/luv/ on August 29, 2014]

So, we share these stories about this successful company because stories help us understand how SC has been and might be applied. Here's how Philip Condit, chairman and chief executive officer of the Boeing Company from 1996 to 2003, describes Herb Kelleher, founder of Southwest Airlines, and this idea of storytelling:

If you go back to tribal behavior...one of the most critical people in any tribe was the shaman, the fundamental storyteller. Keep in mind, their job was not one of historical accuracy. Instead their job was to tell stories that influenced and guided behavior. Stories were modified in order to achieve the appropriate kind of culture. I've watched Herb tell stories: he watches the reaction of people and his story then takes on new and different nuances depending upon his audience and the reaction he is hoping for. You see, stories are powerful because we remember them. I think Herb is Southwest's shaman; he is the storyteller, and those stories get repeated and retold and they form the fabric of the Southwest culture. (Freiberg & Freiberg, 1997, p. 164)

As we ponder the above, and the examples to follow, we should be mindful of our earlier description of leadership as a process through which an individual influences a group of individuals to achieve a common goal. Telling stories is apparently a method of affixing those goals in not just the minds of the members of the organization, but also their hearts...their culture. That is the purpose of the stories and statements that follow, to enable you to have a memory that will positively affect your leadership, as you reflect from the inside-out, while taking the logs out of your eyes to enable your ability to see clearly to lead others through principles, people and purpose. Salient points to remember are provided in italics along with descriptions of how Southwest Airlines models those points.

Seeing Clearly...Principles

• *Clear values*—Although these values are not officially rank-ordered, probably in practice they actually are. Safety is first. Then our next priority is getting the job done, and done well, for our Customers. That is driven by our Warrior Spirit. Yet we don't want to give our all without a Servant's Heart, expressed with a Fun-LUVing [sic] Attitude. Having fun is part of our culture. (Blanchard & Barrett, 2011, p. 91)

• *Make principles second nature*—Profitability, low cost, family, fun, and love are key principles deeply embedded within the culture and shared and practiced by the people. (Freiberg & Freiberg, 1997, p. 172)

• *Uncompromising principles, whether internal or external*—There should be no difference whatsoever between your principles and values when delivering internal Customer Service versus external Customer Service. (Blanchard & Barrett, 2011, p. 69)

• *Prioritize what is important*—You don't have to know the mission word for word if you're an Employee—although most can probably quote it to you—as long as you know that the number-one expectation is that you will practice The Golden Rule every day in a loving way. (Blanchard & Barrett, 2011)

• *Everyone is a leader*—At Southwest Airlines, although we have Manager titles, we prefer to use the word Leader because we want all our People to realize they have the potential to be a Leader; they can make a positive difference in anyone's work and life, regardless of whether they are in a management position or not. (Blanchard & Barrett, 2011, p. 2)

• *Love, not techniques, is the answer*—Without love, techniques are simply another form of sophisticated manipulation with which we exploit people. If there is an overarching reason for Southwest Airlines' success, it is that the company has spent far more time since 1971 focused on loving people than on the development of new management techniques. The tragedy of our time is that we've got it backwards. We've learned to love techniques and use people. (Freiberg & Freiberg, 1997, p. 325)

Seeing Clearly…People as hired hearts

• *Considering people as hired hearts breeds trust, improved performance* - I [Colleen Barrett as President of Southwest Airlines] say to folks every day, "The rules are guidelines. I can't sit in Dallas, Texas, and write a rule for every single scenario you're going to run into. You're out there. You're dealing with the public. You can tell in any given situation when a rule should be bent or broken. You can tell because it's simply the right thing to do in the situation you are facing." When our People [sic] realize they can be trusted and they're not going to get called on the carpet because they bend or break a rule while taking care of a Customer [sic]—that's when they want to do their best. Our People understand that as long as the Customer Service decisions they make are not illegal, unethical, or immoral, they are free to do the right thing while using their best judgment—even if that means bending or breaking a rule or a procedure in the process. (Blanchard & Barrett, 2011, pp. 102-103)

• *Leaders are supportive of their people*—For almost four decades Herb and I [Colleen Barrett] have said that our purpose in life as Senior Leaders with Southwest Airlines is to support our People. (Blanchard & Barrett, 2011, p. 77)

• *Clearly seeing the value of your people*—Working at our Company is what our Employees do, but it's not who they are. They are altruistic People with huge hearts and a deep passion for making a positive difference where they live and work. (Blanchard & Barrett, 2011, p. 60)

• *Burnout and turnover are minimized when people are viewed as hired hearts*—We're so proud of our consistently low turnover rate. Combined voluntary and involuntary turnover has hovered around 5 percent for the past 25 years, and our voluntary turnover rate has always been 3 percent or less. This is truly incredible when you realize that turnover for the transportation industry as a whole has been in the double digits for the last decade, with peaks ranging around the 20 percent mark. (Blanchard & Barrett, 2011, p. 35)

• *Treat people right and they will treat the customer right*—We proudly draw a pyramid on the chalkboard and tell them: You are at the top of the pyramid. You are the most important Person to us. Therefore, I am going to spend 80 percent of my time treating you with Golden Rule behavior and trying to make sure that you have an enjoyable work environment where you feel good about what you do, about yourself and about your position within this Company. But if I do that, what I want in exchange is for you to do the same thing by offering our Passengers—who are our second Customer in terms of priority—the same kind of warmth, caring, and fun spirit. (Blanchard & Barrett, 2011, p. 29)

• *Prompt and caring acknowledgement warms the hearts of followers*—For Colleen [Barrett], giving and acknowledging are not just about buying any old gift and sending it off. Giving is about touching the heart of the recipient, about individualizing the gift. As a result, people feel cared about and important. Consider this from a Southwest pilot: "I'd been with Southwest for two years and I had cancer. The first time I was out for three months, when they removed a kidney. After about six weeks, we received a big package from Herb and Colleen. It was a big cheesecake and some dooda dooda [sic] stuff and it was the first major representation that in this company nobody is forgotten…When I was out the second time I was out for nine months, the same thing happened, different package. We know this is a business and chances are these gifts were a part of a bigger system. But the point is, the company cared enough to put in place all the expense and the resources to make it happen. I ask myself how can a company of twenty-five thousand people, and somebody at Colleen's level, remember people so specifically? And I know that I am not the only one. It happens to a lot of people." (Freiberg & Freiberg, 1997, p. 163)

• *Appropriate celebrations spark passion*—Celebration enhances our humanity. Without celebration, we are robbed of the life and vitality that energizes the human spirit. Latent and undeveloped though it may be, there is within our nature as human beings an inherent need to sing, dance, love, laugh, mourn, tell stories, and celebrate. Whether we are talking about people in Africa, Australia, Asia, Europe, or the Americas, there is no culture in the world that doesn't embrace some form of festivity. To deny our need to celebrate is to deny a part of what it means to be human. Celebration provides an opportunity for building relationships. It gives us a sense of history while helping to envision the future. Celebration helps reduce stress and inspires motivation and reenergizes people. (Freiberg & Freiberg, 1997, pp. 177-185)

• *Hired hearts will serve the customer in a like manner*—Southwest people don't view customers as categories or objects. They view customers as sacred thous [sic] who should be treated with dignity. When a customer is a category, you say, "I'm sorry, there is nothing more I can do for you." When the customer is a sacred thou, you scour the gate area for the lost teddy bear; you park his car when he's running late for a flight; you get out your credit card and pay for her ticket when she's lost her purse; and yes, you even take him off the streets and give him a job. In exercising this form of leadership, Southwest has found that people become healthier, wiser, freer, and more human. (Freiberg & Freiberg, 1997, p. 316)

• *Union leadership and representatives are people too*—We treat all as family, including outside union representatives. We walk into the room not as adversaries but as working on something together. Our attitude is that we should both do what's good for the company…[Unions] have their constituency, their customer base. We respect that. We have a great relationship with the Teamsters and they have a reputation for being tough negotiators. We try to stress with everybody that we really like partnerships. (Gittell, 2003, p. 165)

- *Wary succession planning bequeaths lasting legacy*—"I [Kelleher] thought about who would be my successor very seriously for quite some time. My biggest concern was that I wanted someone who would be respectful of Southwest's culture and would be the sort of person who was altruistic in nature. I think Jim [Parker] and Colleen [Barrett] fit that." Kelleher chose long-time colleague Jim Parker to succeed him as CEO and long-time colleague Colleen Barrett to succeed him as president and chief operating officer. In selecting Barrett, Kelleher also left Southwest with the legacy of having the first top woman executive in the U.S. airline industry. About breaking this barrier, Barrett says with characteristic humility: "It's not anything I ever aspired to…All I ever really wanted to do all my life was enjoy what I do, and I obviously do that. But since all the coverage on this transition has come out, I have been amazed at how many women I have heard from that I don't know. So obviously it's a bigger thing than I would have thought. The glass ceiling has never been an issue for me at Southwest Airlines, so I've never particularly thought of that. But I have heard really big-dog people saying how great it is. It makes me feel great for women. It's kind of humbling." (Gittell, 2003, p. 69)

Seeing Clearly…Purpose is Understood, Communicated and Aligned with Organization

- *Clearly articulated purpose that the organization takes to heart* - To him [Herb Kelleher as CEO of Southwest Airlines], once everybody knew where we were going, what we wanted to accomplish, and what our values were, he always worked for our People and our Customers. (Blanchard & Barrett, 2011, p. 96)

- *Understanding "why" your organization exists*—We're in the Customer Service business—we just happen to provide airline transportation. (Blanchard & Barrett, 2011, p. 66). A higher purpose is something that takes precedence over any short-term goal like profit. (Blanchard & Barrett, 2011, p. 64)

- *Rewards can be negative*—I had to let a personal staff member go because she did not display Golden Rule behavior with her peers. She played well "up" the ladder, so to speak, but not as well with folks she perceived to be at or below her position level. Her skills were top notch—it took two people to replace her—and it was very difficult for me. But obviously it had to be done. (Blanchard & Barrett, 2011, p. 11)

- *Rewards can celebrate success*—We have a small Internal Customer Care Team that, together with personal staff, helps the Executive Office keep track of every Employee's birthday, Company anniversary, the birth of children, and other important events. This Team makes sure that cards go out for nearly every occasion. We just believe in accentuating the positive and celebrating People's successes. (Blanchard & Barrett, 2011, p. 7)

- *Align celebrations to purpose*—Leaders raise people to higher levels of motivation by showing them how their individual contributions are linked to the major purposes of the organization. This is done by acknowledging people's contributions in celebrations, publishing feats in *LUV Lines*, and by simple "thank yous" that say, "What you did made a difference." (Freiberg & Freiberg, 1997, p. 313)

• *Align operational structure with purpose*—Southwest discovered multiple ways to speed the turnaround of its aircraft at the gate, seeking to fulfill its purpose of frequent, low-cost service. First, Southwest used only one aircraft type—the Boeing 737. Southwest standardized cockpit configurations as much as possible to minimize extra training requirements for its pilots. Second, where available, Southwest uses less congested airports to avoid disrupting flight operations and to maximize aircraft time in the air. Third, to speed turnarounds, Southwest offered limited services, specifically no in-flight meals—only beverages and snacks—and did not transfer baggage to other airlines. These practices reduced costs and turnaround time by eliminating the need for software to sort and hold seating assignments, and also printing and verifying boarding passes. (Gittell, 2003, p. 22)

Chapter 6

EPILOGUE

Being a leader is truly a journey. One wonder's if it is possible to make it, as there will always be challenges of which to be concerned. As one destination is obtained, a new one appears on the horizon. Like any journey, however, it is important for the traveler to clearly see the destination they pursue, the means of getting to that place, and the environment or media in which their journey occurs. The concept of Seeing Clearly begins with a search within the individual, establishing ethical principles at the core. Principles are the foundation upon which the aspects of people and purpose are combined within the organization. It is, therefore, essential that we take the time to consider the source for the principles we hold dear. Leaders influence people to accomplish a purpose, and together, principles, people and purpose must be in alignment for an organization to prosper, not only in the present, but also in the uncharted future. It is my desire that within this work, you have obtained a fresh perspective on how to approach your leadership journey. I pray that your organization, no matter how big or how small, will benefit from what you have experienced, and that you will approach those you lead with love.

REFERENCES

Adelson, S. (n.d.). Brainy quote. Retrieved January 18, 2014, from
 http://www.brainyquote.com/quotes/quotes/s/sheldonade356380.html

All services. (2012). *2012 Annual Airline Data*. Retrieved August 06, 2014, from
 http://www.caa.co.uk/docs/80/airline_data/2012Annual/Table_0_1_6_All_Services_
 2012.pdf

Allison, A. M., Maxfield, M. R., Cook, K. D., & Skousen, W. C. (2009). *The real
 Thomas Jefferson*. Malta, ID: National Center for Constitutional Studies.

America's largest private companies. (n.d.). *Forbes*. Retrieved January 18, 2014, from
 http://www.forbes.com/largest-private-
 companies/list/#page:1_sort:0_direction:asc_search:hearst

Ammondson, P. (2001). Beat job burnout. *T+D*, *55*(9), 68–70.

Ashkenas, R., Ulruch, D., Jick, T., & Kerr, S. (2002). *The boundaryless organization*.
 San Francisco: Jossey-Bass.

Barclay, W. (2001). *The Gospel of Luke*. Louisville, Kentucky: Westminster John Knox
 Press.

Bell, C. R. (2002). *Managers as mentors: Building partnerships for learning*. San
 Francisco, CA: Berrett-Koehler Publishers, Inc.

Bethune, G., & Huler, S. (1998). *From worst to first: Behind the scenes of Continental's
 remarkable comeback*. New York: John Wiley Sons, Inc.

Black, J. S., Morrison, A., & Gregersen, H. (1999). *Global explorers: The next
 generation of leaders*. New York: Routledge.

Blackaby, H. T., & Blackaby, R. (2011). *Spititual leadership*. Nashville, TN: B & H Pub.
 Group.

Blanchard, K., & Barrett, C. (2011). *Lead with LUV: A different way to create real
 success*. Upper Saddle River, NJ: FT Press.

Block, P. (2000). *Flawless consulting: A guide to getting your expertise used*. San Francisco, CA: Jossey-Bass/Pfeiffer.

Bluedorn, A. C., Kaufman, C. F., & Lane, P. M. (1992). How many things do you like to do at once? An introduction to monochronic and polychronic time. *The Executive*, *6*(4), 17–26.

Bonn, I. (2001). Developing strategic thinking as a core competency. *Management Decision*, *39*(1), 63–70.

Bossidy, L., & Charan, R. (2009). *Execution: The discipline of getting things done*. New York: Crown Business.

Bradley, C. (2006). Succeeding by (organizational) design. *Decision: Ireland's Business Review*, *11*(1), 4–5.

Buggie, F. D. (1982). Hurdling the barriers to creativity or how to become more like a raccoon. *Nation's Business, January*, 68–69.

Building public trust: Ethics measures in OECD countries. (2000). *OECD Public Management Policy Brief*, *7*(September), 1–6. Retrieved from http://www.oecd.org/mena/governance/35527481.pdf

Bunz, U. K., & Maes, J. D. (1998). Learning excellence: Southwest airlines' approach. *Managing Service Quality*, *8*(3), 163–169.

Burkus, D. (2014). *The myths of creativity*. San Francisco, CA: Jossey-Bass.

Cagliano, R., Caniato, F., Golini, R., Longoni, A., & Micelotta, E. (2011). The impact of country culture on the adoption of new forms of work organization. *International Journal of Operations & Production Management*, *31*(3), 297–323. doi:10.1108/01443571111111937

Carlzon, J. (1989). *Moments of truth*. New York: Harper & Row, Publishers, Inc.

Carr, A. E., & Tang, T. L.-P. (2005). Sabbaticals and employee motivation: Benefits, concerns and implications. *Journal of Education for Business*, (January/February), 160–164.

Carroll, L. (1920). *Alice's adventures in wonderland.* New York. The Macmillan Cmpany.

Carson, B. (2012). *America the beautiful: Rediscovering what made this nation great.* Grand Rapids, Michigan: Zondervan.

Chaleff, I. (2009). *The courageous follower: Standing up to and for our leaders.* San Francisco, CA: Berrett-Koehler Publishers, Inc.

Ciulla, J. B. (2004). *Ethics, the heart of leadership.* Westport: Praeger Publishers.

Clawson, J. G. (2000). The new infocracies : Implications for leadership. *Ivey Business Journal, 64*(5), 76–82.

Cohen, S. L. (2010a). Effective global leadership requires a global mindset. *Industrial and Commercial Training, 42*(1), 3–10. doi:10.1108/00197851011013652

Cohen, S. L. (2010b). Effective global leadership requires a global mindset. *Industrial and Commercial Training, 42*(1), 3–10. doi:10.1108/00197851011013652

Covey, S. R. (1989). *The seven habits of highly effective people.* New York: Simon & Schuster Inc.

Covey, S. R. (1991). The seven habits of highly effective people. *National Medical-Legal Journal, 2*(2), 8. Retrieved from http://www.ncbi.nlm.nih.gov/pubmed/1747433

Daft, R. A. (2010). *Organization theory and design* (10th ed.). Mason, OH: South-Western Cengage Learning.

Davis, K. (1973). Trends in organizational design. *Arizona Business, 20*(9), 3.

Deiser, R. (2011). Creative leadership. *Leadership Excellence, 28*(1), 18.

Delbecq, A. L., & Friedlander, F. (1995). Strategies for personal and family renewal. *Journal of Management Inquiry, 4*(3), 262–269.

Denti, L., & Hemlin, S. (2012). Leadership and innovation in organizations: A systematic review of factors that mediate or moderate the relationship. *International Journal of Innovation Management, 16*(03), 1240007–1– 124007–20. doi:10.1142/S1363919612400075

DePree, M. (2004). *Leadership is an art*. New York: Doubleday.

Device ownership over time. (2014). *Pew Research Internet Project*. Retrieved May 25, 2014, from http://www.pewinternet.org/data-trend/mobile/device-ownership/

Elmer, D. (1993). *Cross-cultural conflict: Building relationships for effective ministry*. Downers Grove, IL: Intervarsity.

Ethics. (2014). *Webster's Third New International Dictionary, Unabridged*.

Frankl, V. E. (2006). *Man's search for meaning*. Boston, MA: Beacon Press.

Freiberg, K., & Freiberg, J. (1997). *Nuts! Southwest Airlines' crazy recipe for business and personal success*. New York: Broadway Books.

Galbraith, J. R. (2002). *Designing organizations: An executive guide to strategy, structure, and process*. San Francisco: Jossey-Bass.

Galston, W. (2010). Commentary: Ethics and character in the U.S. Presidency. *Presidential Studies Quarterly*, *40*(1), 90–101. doi:10.1111/j.1741-5705.2009.03735.x

Gansberg, M. (1964, March 27). Thirty-eight who saw murder didn't call the police. *New York Times*, p. 27. New York.

Gerstein, M. S., & Shaw, R. B. (2008). Organizational bystanders. *People and Strategy*, *31*(1), 47–54.

Gittell, J. H. (2003). *The Southwest Airlines way*. New York: McGraw-Hill.

Gryskiewicz, S. S. (1999). *Positive turbulence: Developing climates for creativity, innovation, and renewal*. San Francisco, CA: Jossey-Bass, Inc.

Gudykunst, W., & Kim, Y. (2002). *Communicating with strangers: An approach to intercultural communication* (4th ed.). Boston, MA: McGraw-Hill.

Guinnes, O., Mooney, V., & Thorp, K. (2000). *When no one sees: The importance of character in an age of image*. Colorado Springs, CO: Navpress.

Hall, E. T. (1959). *The silent language*. Westport: Greenwood Publishing Group, Inc.

Hall, E. T. (1960). The silent language in overseas business. *Harvard Business Review*, *38*(3), 87–96.

Hammonds, K. H. (2002, June). The strategy of the fighter pilot. *Fast Company*. Retrieved from http://www.fastcompany.com/44983/strategy-fighter-pilot

Handy, C. (1989). *The age of unreason*. Boston, MA: Harvard Business School Press.

HCSB Study Bible, Holman Christian Standard Bible: God's word for life. (2010). Nashville, TN: Holman Bible Publishers.

Hellreigel, D., & Slocum Jr., J. W. (1973). Organizational design - A contingency approach. *Business Horizons*, *16*(2), 59–68.

Hitt, M. A., Miller, C. C., & Colella, A. (2009). *Organizational behavior: A strategic approach* (2nd ed.). Pennsylvania State University: John Wiley Sons, Inc.

Hofstede, G., & Peterson, M. F. (2000). Culture: National values and organizational practices. In *Handbook of organizational culture and climate* (pp. 401–416).

Hoover, C. (2010). The strategic communication plan. *FBI Law Enforcement Bulletin*, *August*, 16–21.

House, R. J., Hanges, P. J., Javidan, M., Dorfman, P. W., & Gupta, V. (2004). *Culture, leadership, and organizations: The GLOBE study of 62 societies*. Thousand Oaks, CA: SAGE Publications Inc.

Hoyes, M. (2014). *Eulogy for 3D assembly*. Yorktown, VA: Speech presented at Grafton High School.

Hoyes, M. B. (2012). *Organizational design: Revisiting Galbraith's star model* (pp. 1–11). Yorktown.

Huntington, S. P. (1996). *The clash of civilizations and the remaking of world order*. New York: Simon & Schuster.

Jacobs, G. A. (2006). Servant leadership and follower commitment. In *Proceedings of the 2006 Servant Leadership Research Roundtable* (pp. 1–16). Retrieved from http://www.regentuniversityonline.com/acad/global/publications/sl_proceedings/2006/jacobs.pdf

Joas, H. (2000). *The genesis of values*. Chicago, IL: The University of Chicago Press.

John McAllister Schofield quotes. (n.d.). *ThinkExist.Com Quotations Online*. Retrieved May 24, 2014, from http://en.thinkexist.com/quotes/john_mcallister_schofield/

Keidel, R. W. (1995). *Seeing organizaitonal patterns: A new theory and language of organizational design*. Washington, D.C.: BeardBooks.

Kelley, R. E. (1992). *The power of followership*. New York: Doubleday Dell Publishing Group, Inc.

Kelly, N. (2007). Why trust matters. *Leadership Excellence*, *24*(8), 13.

Khurana, R. (2002). *Searching for a corporate savior: The irrational quest for charismatic CEOs*. Princeton, NJ: Princeton University Press.

King, M. L. (1958). Paul's letter to American Christians, sermon delivered to the Commission on Ecumenical Missions and Relations, United Presbyterian Church, U.S.A. Pittsburgh, PA. Retrieved from http://mlk-kpp01.stanford.edu/primarydocuments/Vol6/3June1958Paul'sLettertoAmericanChristinas,SermonDeliveredtotheCommissiononEcumenicalMissionsandRelations,UnitedPresbyterianChurch,USA.pdf

Kolditz, T. (2014). Why you lead determines how well you lead. *Harvard Business Review*. Retrieved July 24, 2014, from http://blogs.hbr.org/2014/07/why-you-lead-determines-how-well-you-lead/

Kowitt, B. (2013). The big handoff at Hearst. *Fortune*, *168*(8), 136–144.

Kroeber, A. L., & Kluckhohn, C. (1952). Culture: A critical review of concepts and definitions. *Peabody Museum of American Archaeology and Ethnology*, *XLVII*(1), 159–190.

Kuczmarski, S. S., & Kuczmarski, T. D. (1995). *Values-based leadership*. Englewood Cliffs, NJ: Prentice Hall, Inc.

Lanre-Abass, B. (2008). The crisis of leadership in Nigeria and the imperative of a virtue ethics. *Philosophia Africana*, *II*(2), 117–140.

Laurie, D. L., & Harreld, B. J. (2013). Six ways to sink a growth initiative. *Harvard Business Review, July*, 1–10.

Levitt, T. (1975, Sept/Oct). Marketing myopia. *Harvard Business Review, 53*, 1–25.

Lewis, C. S. (1980). *Mere Christianity*. New York: HarperCollins Publishers.

Liedtka, J. (1998). Strategic thinking: Can it be taught? *Long Range Planning, 31*(1), 120–129. doi:10.1016/S0024-6301(97)00098-8

Lillrank, P., Shani, A. B., & Lindberg, P. (2001). Continuous improvement: Exploring alternative organizational designs. *Total Quality Management, 12*(1), 41–55. doi:10.1080/09544120020010084

Lin, Z. (John), Zhao, X., Ismail, K. M., & Carley, K. M. (2006). Organizational design and restructuring in response to crises: Lessons from computational modeling and real-world cases. *Organization Science, 17*(5), 598–618. doi:10.1287/orsc.1060.0210

List of OECD Member countries - Ratification of the Convention on the OECD. (n.d.). *OECD*. Retrieved May 31, 2014, from http://www.oecd.org/about/membersandpartners/list-oecd-member-countries.htm

Lyon, A. (2007). Moral motives and policy actions: The case of Dag Hammarskjöld at the United Nations. *Public Integrity, 9*(1), 79–95. doi:10.2753/PIN1099-9922090105

Marquardt, M., & Berger, N. (2000). *Global leaders for the 21st century*. Albany, NY: State University of New York.

Maslach, C., & Leiter, M. P. (1997). *The truth about burnout*. San Francisco, CA: Jossey-Bass.

McCall, M., & Hollenbeck, G. (2002). *Developing global executives*. Boston: Harvard Business School.

McCaskey, M. B. (1974). An introduction to organiational design. *California Management Review, 17*(2), 13–20.

McCaskey, M. B. (1974). An introduction to organizational design. *California Management Review, 17*(2), 13–20.

Mendonca, M. (2001). Preparing for ethical leadership in organizations. *Canadian Journal of Administrative Sciences, 18*(4), 266–276.

Michalko, M. (2001). *Cracking creativity: The secrets of creative genius.* Berkeley, CA: Ten Speed Press.

Michalko, M. (2006). *Thinkertoys: A handbook of creative-thinking techniques.* Berkeley, CA: Ten Speed Press.

Michelangelo. (n.d.). On the painting of the Sistine Chapel (translated by John Addington Symonds). *All Poetry.* Retrieved August 02, 2014, from http://allpoetry.com/On-The-Painting-Of-The-Sistine-Chapel

Mihelic, K. K., Lipicnik, B., & Tekavcic, M. (2010). Ethical leadership. *International Journal of Management and Information Systems, 14*(5), 31–41.

Miller, C. (1995). *The empowered leader: 10 keys to servant leadership.* Nashville, TN: Broadman & Holman Publishers.

Moral. (2014). *Webster's Third New International Dictionary, Unabridged.*

Morgan, G. (2006). *Images of organization.* Thousand Oaks, CA: SAGE Publications.

Muller, W. (1999). *Sabbath: Finding rest, renewal, and delight in our busy lives.* New York: Bantam Books.

Nadler, D. A., & Tushman, M. L. (1999). The organization of the future: Strategic imperatives and core competencies for the 21st century. *Organizational Dynamics, 28*(1), 45–60.

Nelson, M. C. (2000). Facing the future: Intellectual capital of our workforce. *Vital Speeches of the Day, 67*(5), 138–143.

Northouse, P. G. (2010). *Leadership theory and practice* (5th ed.). Thousand Oaks, CA: SAGE Publications Inc.

O'Neil, J. (2004). *The paradox of success.* New York: Penguin Group (USA) Inc.

Oster, G. (2011). *The light prize: Perspectives on Christian innovation*. Virginia Beach, VA: Positive Signs Media.

Overholt, M. H. (1997). Flexible organizations : Using organizational design as a competitive advantage. *HR. Human Resource Planning, 20*(1), 22–32.

Overholt, M. H., Connally, G. E., Harrington, T. C., & Lopez, D. (2000). The strands that connect: An empirical assessment of how organizational design links employees to the organization. *The Human Resource Planning, 23*(2), 38–51.

Parjanen, S. (2012). Experiencing creativity in the organization: From individual creativity to collective creativity. *Interdisciplinary Journal of Information, Knowledge, and Management, 7*, 109–128.

Pfeffer, J. (1994). Competitive advantage through people. *California Management Review, 36*(2), 9–28.

Plinio, A. J., Young, J. M., & Lavery, L. M. (2010). The state of ethics in our society: A clear call for action. *International Journal of Disclosure and Governance, 7*(3), 172–197. doi:10.1057/jdg.2010.11

Prilipko, E. V., Antelo, A., & Henderson, R. L. (2011). Rainbow of followers' attributes in a leadership process. *International Journal of Management and Information Systems, 15*(2), 79–94.

principle. (2014). *Webster's Third New International Dictionary, Unabridged*. Retrieved June 07, 2014, from http://unabridged.merriam-webster.com

Robinson, K. (2006). Why schools kill creativity. *Red Tape*, #3.

Rosen, R., Digh, P., Singer, M., Philips, C., & Phillips, C. (2000). *Global literacies: Lessons on business leadership and national cultures*. New York: Simon & Schuster.

Rothwell, W. J. (2005). *Effective succession planning: Ensuring leadership continuity and building talent from within* (3rd ed.). New York: AMACOM.

Rothwell, W. J. (2010). The future of succession planning. *T+D, 64*(9), 50–54.

Sanders, T. I. (1998). *Strategic thinking and the new science*. New York: The Free Press.

Sarangi, S., & Srivastava, R. K. (2012). Impact of organizational culture and communication on employee engagement: An investigation of Indian private banks. *South Asian Journal of Management*, *19*(3), 18–32.

Schaufeli, W. B., Leiter, M. P., & Maslach, C. (2009). Burnout: 35 years of research and practice. *Career Development International*, *14*(3), 204–220. doi:10.1108/13620430910966406

Schwab, K. (2014). *The global competitiveness report 2013-2014*. (K. Schwab, Ed.) (Full Data .). World Economic Forun.

Senge, P. M. (2006). *The fifth discipline: The art & practice of the learning organization.* New York: Doubleday.

Sharpe, M. E. (1981). *International Studies of Management & Organizations*, *X*(4), 15–41.

Sheldon Adelson. (2013). *Forbes*. Retrieved January 18, 2014, from http://www.forbes.com/profile/sheldon-adelson/

Sinek, S. (2011). *Start with why: How great leaders inspire everyone to take action.* New York: Penguin Group Inc.

Skousen, W. C. (2006). *The 5000 year leap*. Malta, ID: National Center for Constitutional Studies.

Skousen, W. C. (2007). *The making of America*. Malta, ID: National Center for Constitutional Studies.

Southwest Airlines Co. (2014). *Fortune*. Retrieved August 29, 2014, from http://fortune.com/company/luv/

Tedesco, T. J., & Farquhason, B. (2012). Unleashing the power of "why." *Printing Impressions*, *55*(5), 66–69.

Toffler, A. (1971). *Future shock.* New York: Bantam Books.

Utterback, J. M. (1996). *Mastering the dynamics of innovation.* Boston, MA: Harvard Business School Press.

Warden, J. A., & Russell, L. A. (2002). *Winning in fasttime*. Montgomery, AL: Venturist Publishing.

Watts, T. (2014). Lewis Latimer. *American History*. Retrieved May 31, 2014, from http://0-americanhistory2.abc-clio.com.library.regent.edu/

What is distracted driving? (n.d.). *U.S. Department of Transportation*. Retrieved April 30, 2014, from http://www.distraction.gov/content/get-the-facts/facts-and-statistics.html

Willard, D. (2002). *Renovation of the heart: Putting on the character of Christ*. Colorado Springs, CO: NAVPRESS.

Winston, B. E. (2002). *Be a leader for God's sake*. Virginia Beach, VA: School of Leadership Studies, Regent University.

Winston, B. E. (2009). Agapao leadership. *Inner Resources for Leaders*, 1–6.

Winston, B. E., & Patterson, K. (2006). An integrative definition of leadership. *International Journal of Leadership Studies*, *1*(2), 6–66. Retrieved from http://regentuniversity.org/acad/global/publications/ijls/new/vol1iss2/winston_patter son.doc/winston_patterson.pdf

Wrzesniewski, A., Schwartz, B., Cong, X., Kane, M., Omar, A., & Kolditz, T. (2014). Multiple types of motives don't multiply the motivation of West Point cadets. *Proceedings of the National Academy of Sciences of the United States of America*, 1–6. doi:10.1073/pnas.1405298111

Wuellner, F. S. (1998). *Feed my shepherds*. Nashville: Upper Room Books.

Yukl, G. (2010). *Leadership in organizations* (7th ed.). Upper Saddle River, NJ: Prentice Hall.

Zappella, C. (n.d.). Michelangelo's ceiling of the Sistine Chapel. *SmartHistory*.

Zweifel, T. D. (2003). *Culture clash: Managing the global high-performance team*. New York: SelectBooks.

INDEX

ABOUT THE AUTHOR

Dr. Michael Hoyes has journeyed far to pen this book. During that journey, he has experienced deep valleys and mountain top experiences. With a career spanning more than 30 years in the United States Air Force, he has flown in combat and was an instructor at the elite United States Fighter Weapons School, giving to others the tactical and technical savvy to survive in combat. He has commanded two units during his military career and was one of several architects of the Strategic Air Campaign employed during Operation DESERT STORM. One of his favorite recollections is of a going away function where he was told "you love us more than you love yourself." That single accolade means more to him than being twice selected as a Lance P. Sijan Leadership Award winner at one of his assignments. Though no longer serving on active duty in the USAF, Dr. Hoyes continues to serve the nation that he loves by working a full-time, demanding job as a consultant for the defense community. With the full support of his family, friends and colleagues, he pursued and earned his Doctor of Strategic Leadership degree through Regent University in 2014. He would tell you that his journey in understanding leadership is far from over. Dr. Hoyes is eager to share and converse with others who seek to comprehend leadership: what it means and how to grow and apply it. He currently resides in Yorktown, Virginia with his wife Claudia, and together they have been blessed with four children and four grandchildren.

Made in the USA
Lexington, KY
30 April 2015